101 Business Lessons From A Recovering Accountant

"Business Lessons from my Window Cleaner,
Margaret Thatcher, George Clooney and many more"

Sep '21

Kate,

Hope you enjoy the read.

Neil

Neil O' Brien

SPECIAL THANKS

Special thanks to:

My amazing publisher, Orla Kelly. I can safely say that without her, this book would not be in your hands right now. If you are interested in publishing a book, I highly recommend Orla and you can reach her at Orla Kelly Publishing.

Jean O'Sullivan of Red Pen Edits my editor, did a great job in knocking the rough edges off this book and helped make the content flow better and for this I am very grateful to her.

A big 'thank you' to my mastermind group led by Paull Newsome. Up to May 2017, a rough draft of this book was sitting on a desk in my office gathering dust for the previous 12 months. In May I committed to my group to have the book printed and in my hands by early August. I collected that first print copy of my book on 4th August. I know that without my mastermind group and my commitment to them this book would not have been printed as quickly as it was. Many thanks to each and every one of you for helping me make and keep that commitment.

A big thank you to everybody who read an advance copy of this book and provided me with a review (these are at the front of the book).

These reviewers were Sharon O'Dwyer, Seamus English, Paull Newsome, Paul Skuse, Nadeem Igbal, Mark Tanner, Florin Lungu, John Daly, Fiona Donnelly, Dean, Colin Johnson, Adrian Jardine, Meredith Viguers, Christina Gilberti, Paul Widdershovena and Donal O'Callaghan.

I am very grateful to Perry Marshall, a Guru not just in 80:20 but also in pay per click ads (both Google and Facebook), who wrote a fabulous foreword for this book.

Another special thank you to Richard Koch, author of the bestselling and original Bible on the subject of a 80:20 "The 80:20 Principle",who sent me a lovely review.

I am also very grateful to all my friends and family who have helped me, not just in producing this book, but in my entrepreneurial journey since 2003.

Even after this book is published, I am sure that the 'star of the show' will be Rocky, my sister's Jack Russell dog who features in this book. What Rocky lacks in rabbit catching skills, he makes up for by providing inspiration and material for numerous stories in this book.

Neil O'Brien, September 2017

FOREWORD BY

PERRY MARSHALL

The real title of Neil's book should probably be "20% of your customers are losing you money. You just don't know who they are." And while there are a number of great 80/20 books, this one drives this particular point home better than the others.

Very little in your business is really the way you think it is, and if you have the courage to put on your "80/20 X-Ray Vision Glasses" and see the real truth, you will be in for a shock. Most people do not know the truth.

The truth is, you are making red-ink mistakes with your pricing strategy, your marketing, your customer service and your product lines. And almost nobody realizes that nearly every business on the planet is ridden with money-sucking profit burning customers. That is the truth.

But as a very wise man once said, the truth shall set you free, and if you're willing to do a real 80/20 study of your business you may find yourself incredibly liberated.

Some ways of approaching 80/20 will dramatically improve your sales. Others will dramatically slash your expenses. You will likely find that you can make money serving fewer customers than you are now; and that you can put bigger profits in your pocket, and pay yourself more, with less sales.

This is counterintuitive. But everything about 80/20 is counterintuitive. And you may also find in this book that...

- Social Media is losing you money
- You are taping dollar bills or euros to every single unit you ship, for some of your product line
- Key employees are losing you money
- Key advertising channels are losing you money
- Your accountant is losing you money
- You are probably UNDER-using email
- You are probably ignoring, neglecting or shortchanging some of your most PROFITABLE and LOYAL customers

...and you almost certainly need to take a cue from the Irish girl who kissed George Clooney.

Speaking of Irish, Neil hails from southwest Ireland, which is my favorite corner of the world. And if you're ever in Cork and if you can demonstrate to Neil that you really read and absorbed his book, you'll almost certainly be able to persuade him to join you for a drink at {that cool pub we went to} and perhaps a hike as well on the hills and cliffs of the Irish coast.

Neil may be too busy to meet up with you for free. But he will almost certainly do all that stuff if you pay his fee. And his fee will be worth every penny.

When you're in Cork, say hi to him for me. And perhaps also take a drive up to the Dingle Peninsula, climb Mount Brandon and visit the Great Blasket Island.

But whatever you do, don't ignore his book.

Perry Marshall
Chicago, USA
Author, *80/20 Sales & Marketing, Ultimate Guide to Google AdWords,* and *Ultimate Guide to Facebook Advertising.*

REVIEWS

"This is a must-read for any business owner. But only if you want to **multiply your profits and cash.**"
Richard Koch, author of the million-copy bestseller *The 80/20 Principle.*

Sharon O'Dwyer, Nutritional Therapist.
www.yourpracticalnutrition.ie

Neil's book *'101 Business Lessons From A Recovering Accountant'* excited me. As a small business owner on a tight budget with little time to invest in either learning about how to grow my business or actually doing it, this book gave me some **extremely insightful** and **simple tools** that I know I can use straight away to market my business more effectively. What I particularly loved about this book was......**it's hilarious!**

Neil has an **outrageous sense of humour** and uses tons of examples I could immediately relate to, to really make it easy to understand how to apply a tool to my business. This is a book I looked forward to returning to as it had the effect of thoroughly entertaining me but by the end of a particular section, I totally understood, say, 'how to market effectively with no money' (just one of the sections in his book) using simple tools I could apply immediately.

Like a light bulb going on I saw clearly why some efforts I was making to grow my business were delivering no results and how a few easy tweaks could make a huge difference.

Really, this book has already **saved me money** and may be the only grounded toolkit I need to grow my business to the next level… and giving me a hugely enjoyable and funny read at the same time!

Neil's so witty and human in it, I loved reading it, it's simple to understand and after reading it, I felt inspired to do some of the things you suggest. **Brilliant, Brilliant!!**

Seamus English, Contract Business Solutions.

When I sat down to read this book by Neil O'Brien, I knew it would be interesting. What I didn't realise was that it would also be entertaining. When you look at the section headers - 80:20, selling price, marketing, mind-set, finance, sales and customer service and general – you would think ...ok, this is all going to be interesting and practical stuff, especially to a business owner.

It is more than this, however. Neil tells stories throughout and gives many practical examples that keep your mind alert and make you want to read on. As I went through each section, I found myself relating everything to my own business. His points are supported by facts and figures, and told with a sense of humour.

His **passion for the topics** is evident and makes you seriously think about how you could and should implement his points into your business. It all makes sense. I found myself left in no doubt as to what I need to do, in a few areas. No more thinking, **increase your profits**.......just do it!

Paull Newsome, Associate CEO, Christian Simpson Enterprises Ltd.

"Neil has clearly experienced 80/20 in all sorts of businesses and made a valuable study which he has turned into solid practical advice that ALL Business Owners should heed and implement"

Paul Skuse, Creative Director, Figura Visualisation.

"Packed with Pareto and Profits. Neil's fast and punchy style gives you a huge array of **powerful key messages in record time** and the tools to take action for immediate results. More of a personal sales and business coach than a book... this **must-read** will be a constant companion as you grow your business."

Nadeem Iqbal – Accountant and Tax Advisor' Associate of Institute of Financial Accountants and the member of TaxAssist Accountants.

Neil lives his life on 80:20 Principle. Neil helps his clients not only to grow their sales but he also possesses some magical skills to double their profits even with the current level of sales. Numbers in any business are like scores in the sports: you cannot win a game without knowing your scores.

In this book, Neil helps you not only how to understand your scores, but like a coach, he also motivates you to take the appropriate actions.

Neil's uniqueness lies in the cross section of the 80:20 principle. He exposes different levels of the principles and explains **'whales' and 'super whales'** under this cross section. Neil continuously emphasizes the importance of 20% of customers and shows you the tactics to either transform the other 80% into profitable customers or simply get rid of them.

The 80:20 principle helps you to get a better understanding of your existing clients too. Neil demonstrates how to identify a 20% valued group of clients and then another 20% prime group of clients within the valued group which gives you an opportunity to **develop prime products for them to increase your profitability.**

In this book, you will meet Neil as an **accountant, a financial advisor, a marketer, a customer services coach and a business mentor.** He takes you through a full journey of sales and growth process, from probing into your existing numbers to identify the profitable opportunities, to guide on crafting the prime products, to evolving marketing strategies and your own personal development to serve the profitable group with margin rich repeat sales.

This book is all about understanding the **difference between a sale and a profitable sale.** You will get an opportunity to explore deep down into 80:20 principle and find the right niche for your business and then devise and implement a powerful marketing strategy of many tested and well-proven tactics to increase the profitability of your firm. This book hugely motivates you to take the right and most effective actions towards your profitable firm.

Mark Tanner, MnJ Online Ltd.

"If you are looking for great lessons that can help your business grow, this is a must-read book. This gives the business owner a tremendous amount of information and insights, all simply laid out and written in an easy, conversational style.

It has given me some strategies that I will implement as I know it will for you too."

John Daly, Bear and Bunny Nursery.

"Full of **great pearls of wisdom** on a range of topics I needed to hear and they're applicable to any business. Neil has a great entertaining writing style, a very easy read (I read it so quickly I think I need to read it again).

If you've never heard of 80/20 and how it can help your business, read this book, it will make so much sense. If you think you know all about 80/20, then I dare you to read and not come away with a much better understanding of how it can be applied. **A fantastic read**."

Florin Lungu, Business Coach.

"A must-read book. This book is full of Neil's expertise as result of years of experience in business consulting working with entrepreneurs in all fields. You will plug-in to the best business consulting mentor that I know. A very smart way to learn how to take your business to the next level without making all the mistakes yourself.

It feels like reading all the good stories from seven books condensed in one. I found it packed with learning and straight forward information especially around the 80:20 principle explained so a child will get it. The short and funny stories make the point and unfold the learning beautifully."

Fiona Donnelly, Nexus Consulting.

That clients are *not* born equal is one of the strongest messages I've absorbed from Neil's book. The lens in this book clearly hones in on the principle of 80/20 by discussing how business owners can integrate its fundamentals into a robust sales mentality and practice. It's a given that all clients deserve the same levels of respect, but from a sales perspective all that glitters is not necessarily gold.

The simple fact is that roughly 80% of a client base will generate just 20% of the potential revenue a business experiences – that's a rather sobering thought and flies in the face of conventional advice to treat all customers and clients the same – O'Brien posits that it is *not* an equal playing field, and from his experience, one could surmise that 80% of a company's clients are possibly just shooting the proverbial breeze.

The 80/20 principle itself is not ground-breaking nor novel; but O'Brien's approach to utilizing its value in terms of managing clients, sales, and business growth, is stellar. His professional background in accountancy, entrepreneurship and mentoring is highly evident from this informative read.

Awareness of the 80/20 basis in itself is valuable, but what is a business to do to with that nugget in order to extract the golden geese, or "whales", to borrow O'Brien's language?

He cleverly demonstrates how to assess the current client base relative to their ongoing value, and plan accordingly. **High value clients are the "whales." These are the gold-top 20% of the whole client population**, which equate to a whopping 80% in terms of potential revenue and profit; these are the ones that bring by far, *the* most to the table. Optimizing this client/business relationship not only increases the chances of higher income but also heightens the chances of **attracting new high-paying clients**.

O'Brien's book goes much further than just providing a formulaic process to follow: it digs deeper, outlining ways in which a business owner can take stock of his or her own capabilities through a journey of behavioural reflection.

Carefully probing in a coaching-like manner, the book guides the reader through many scenarios in an attempt to awaken them from self-limiting patterns – how one treats their business is often out of habit, through years of conditioned beliefs. This book reveals how the direction and control of business sales performance can have serious ramifications in terms of potential revenue and work/life balance.

Learning how to streamline sales behaviours and thought-processes in order to grab a larger bite of the pie is ultimately the key to unlocking higher returns. The author has achieved this aim by writing this practical and insightful book, the result of his many years' experience in the field. **A must-read book for all business owners**, from start-ups to established ventures.

Dean, Orchid Computers.

"This book is eye opening and informative – it gives clear and concise information on areas of business that you won't be aware can be improved or even thought possible to achieve. Its simplicity will enable you to implement its ideas immediately and see measurable results

A must read for all aspiring business owners who desire long term growth and survival."

Colin Johnson, Colin Johnson Jewellery.

Having had personal experience of Neil O'Brien's business mentoring, I signed up for his daily anecdotes. They were often stories involving his fearsome Jack Russell 'Rocky', or thoughts and amusing observations on life in general.

The difference with Neil's yarns is that there was always a business moral to the tale. **Useful and eminently applicable** to anyone running their own business, I am glad to say that many of these inspiring stories are contained within the pages of his excellent debut book, '*101 Business Lessons From A Recovering Accountant.*'

The book also covers many other principal areas of good business practice. He is particularly keen on The Pareto Principle, or '80:20 Rule'. With this, he effortlessly unpicks the detail and explains, again with an easy to follow and matter of fact approach, this important business principal, which should become an imperative to all who care about their business.

I can highly recommend this book to either start-ups or those who like me, run a business, but have not necessarily had any formal business training; and **would like to increase their profit margins**, and have a slightly more structured, 'in control' approach.

Adrian Jardine, Managing Director, Alfa-Aid.

If you have never heard of the Pareto Principle you **must** read this book, it will change your business thinking forever. If you have, and you understand 80:20 then you need to read this book as **it will reawaken your thinking and show you more opportunities** already within your business. Neil writes in a very straightforward, often humorous and understandable manner that makes the whole book easy to read and simple to digest. I would recommend it to anyone who wants to improve efficiency and live a better lifestyle.

Meredith Viguers, Owner of 'Let Us Do The Cooking.'

"A simple and practical **approach to maximizing business profits** that doesn't seem daunting. As a small business owner working the numbers of my business can seem overwhelming. In this book Neil has broken it down and explained things in such a way that **I'm actually looking forward to applying the 80:20 rule** to my clients and working the numbers. This book is a must for any business looking to grow!

Christina Giliberti, Owner of CG Online Marketing.

As a client and friend, I have had the direct pleasure of experiencing the power of 80:20 first-hand with Neil at the helm.

This book clearly demonstrates the usefulness of financial analysis and insight. I was amazed that by simply dissecting figures, an accurate picture of the financial health of a business was suddenly apparent. However; what was most empowering, was that the knowledge backed action. Decisions were not just based on whims of the moment, but on actual factual information.

From here, business development decisions such as price increases, development in more affluent markets, and allocations of budget towards sales, were made to propel the business forward.

Not only did we all feel that we had the facts to profit, but we all became more aware of what we needed to do to make this happen. Any change we needed to make could be calculated and used to guide us forward. We felt in control of all our decisions and where they would lead.

Neil has a way of telling stories that links a strong 'numbers' brain with an equally strong 'words' brain. These are easy to read, understand and apply to your own situation. I would refer to this book as a 'profitability self help guide for businesses'. **A delightful and captivating read!**

Donal O'Callaghan, Dynosaor Rokks.

"I had the pleasure of reading Neil's first book when he distributed it daily in memorable increments to his early email circle.

Neil articulates with refreshing simplicity exactly what a beleaguered business owner needs to help him step from the unrewarding drudge of old ways and habits into the sunshine of proactive success-patterns.

All the education you really needed but never received is laid out like a banquet; and whether you take the full course or select favoured morsels to taste, your business acumen will be honed and sharpened; indeed, even your personal day-to-day life-skills will be improved by the nourishment to be enjoyed here.

Neil puts into nutshells what SME owners most need to hear. The book is a treasure trove of the most pertinent principles, solid wisdom, practicality and dogged encouragement. It will rally your resolve, stir your courage and equip you with the tools to analyse the conditions of your business accurately, reason out the most appropriate plan, provide the means of achieving it and inspire you with hope.

He trawls through a subject much hackneyed, and reduces the 'noise' to reveal penetrating truths and nuggets of pure gold that will withstand the test of time in the life of any business, and guide its path from failure towards success. **It is a great book Neil - thanks for writing it.**

Paul Widdershovena, Entrepreneur and fisherman.

Neil O'Brien is a Profit Alchemist. This book is full of practical principles that Neil has used in helping businesses, large and small, to dramatically increase their profits. Once you "get it" you will never look at how you do business the same.

ABOUT THE AUTHOR

He was a management accountant for over 15 years spending time in the U.K, USA and Ireland working for the likes of EMC and Pfizer. He started his own consultancy business in 2003 and has worked with over 250 companies including Centra, Four Star Pizza, EMC, U.C.C., many accountancy practices and various Government agencies. In 2016, several clients saw a jump in profits of between 32% and 54% after just 3 months.

In this book '*101 Business Lessons From A Recovering Accountant,*' you will learn:

- How to increase your prices and NOT lose customers
- The most important step to dramatically increasing profits, yet the most overlooked
- Why 80/20 is such a powerful tool
- How to spot your most profitable whales and change your business for ever
- Steps to ease profit sucking clients out of your business

- Lots of zero cost marketing tips
- How to get a scoreboard in your business to track all your key numbers
- And much more

Neil O'Brien

For a complementary initial analysis of how 80/20 can impact your business, contact Neil@Quantum.ie

Receive a free profit tip every week delivered to your email. Go to Quantum.ie for more details.

For any questions or additional support, Neil can be contacted at Neil@Quantum.ie

https://www.quantum.ie

TABLE OF CONTENTS

SECTION 1

80:20 – THE MOST POWERFUL LESSON IN BUSINESS

The Extraordinary Power of 80:20

The problem with customers is – they are not all the same. Here is a story explaining why… This is the story of how I first stumbled on 80:20 and how it **changed my life forever**.

Many years ago, I worked as an accountant for an electronics firm. They were sub-contractors and made electronic parts which the customer would take to complete and test themselves. The routine work of month end and budgets bored me senseless. What I loved doing was checking to ensure profit margins were being maintained. I loved working out the customer profitability. That meant taking the total sales and costs and dividing it out customer by customer. It was like a mini profit and loss for each customer. You could clearly see which customers were giving you a profit and which ones you were losing money on. Yes, this was hard to accept for the owner, but certain customers were losing them money.

This company had about thirty-six customers. When I had completed the exercise, I sorted them in descending order. On the left-hand side were the most profitable customers and the far right-hand side were the ones who lost you money. When the numbers were finalised, what I saw was quite **EXTRAORDINARY**.

This business had thirty-six customers and just three of them accounted for 91% of the net profit. Fifteen had small profits. The remaining eighteen were all losing money. This was a huge lightbulb moment for me.

It was the most powerful information I had ever seen in business. I was thinking to myself, 'Every business should know this. This can change everything and help drive huge profit growth.'

At that point, I knew my days working as an accountant were numbered. I loved analysing numbers and helping businesses grow profits.

80:20 has been a huge part of my life ever since.

> **If your business has 100 clients, then 20 of them may give you the bulk of your profits.**
> **Of the other 80 clients, many of them will be losing you money.**

How to 80:20 Your Whales…

I have completed 80:20 analysis for dozens of businesses and the trend is always the same – a small number of highly profitable clients (whales) and loads of loss-makers (sardines). In some cases, the whales can account for 150% of profits and they are subsidising loss-makers of 50%.

Even though 80:20 on its own is extraordinary and can transform any business, it gets even better.

In the story above about the electronics company, just three out of their thirty-six customers were giving this business 91% of their total profits. Within those three customers, there was another whale – only one of those three were giving them 60% of their total profits. These are like 'super whale customers.' This is a great example of the levels within 80:20. So when you identify your whales, do the 80:20 again as there will be another whale in there. Let us look at some numbers...

Imagine a business has 100 customers. The 80:20 rule applies so 20 of their customers give 80% of profits. 80:20 applies to these 20 customers so 4 of them (20% X 20%) gives 64% (80% X 80%) of total profits. The 80:20 rule is a guide as sometimes it is 90:10 and other times it is 70:30. The overall principle does not change.

80:20 = 20% of customers give 80% of profits

20% of customers = (20% X 20%) → 64% = (80% X 80%) of total profits

A small number of your customers give you a large portion of your profits.

And within this portion, another small percentage gives a large portion of the profits. Where most businesses miss out on these extra profits is they do not have the high-end deluxe products that these 'super whale' customers want.

The electronics company above is a good example where 3% (1/36) of customers gave that business 55% (91% X 60%).

It was Perry Marshall in his brilliant book, '*80:20 Sales and Marketing*,' who highlighted the layers to 80:20 like the example above. Richard Koch's book '*The 80:20 Principle*' made the point that, 'Your best new customers are your existing ones.'

There is an example in another chapter of a marketing consultant who had an online members' forum with 100 customers paying €100 per month. When he introduced a deluxe mastermind group at €950 per month, 20 of his 'super whale' customers signed up, giving him an extra €228,000 in sales.

> 80:20 has layers to it so within your whale customers are 'super whale' customers. This means just 4% of customers can give you 64% of profits.
> Develop products for them and you can double your profits overnight.

Photocopiers Suck Profits

I have been working with a client using 80:20 techniques, and I have been blown away with what we found. I think we will more than double their net profit in a year, even keeping the current level of sales. If their profit is €100 now; I believe it could be €239 by the end of this year. I will also be helping them grow their sales which will increase profits further, but I am going to leave that to one side for now and focus on the first part – more than doubling their profits based on their current level of sales.

How is that possible? In short, 80:20 is the answer.

What did we do to identify this massive increase? And what lessons are here for your business? What we did was break down their profit and loss, so it does take some number crunching but not a huge amount.

There are two main aspects to this business and the best way to think about it is that they make photocopiers and toners. Overall the business is quite profitable but the owners feel the toners are more profitable than the photocopiers. We took the sales and the costs and split them across the two parts of the business. With some of these, like wages, it is not too difficult as they have reps and other staff allocated to specific parts of the business. For example, admin staff who work on both sides of the business were split 50:50.

When we finished the exercise, the numbers were an eye opener for everybody. While the toners made a profit of €224,000, the photocopiers lost €124,000.

80:20 is the single most powerful principle that you can ever apply to your business.

How is it possible that one part of the business is so profitable while another loses money? This loss happens for a number of reasons. The previous year when working out the selling price of the photocopiers, not all of the related costs were included, like admin, staff, diesel, etc.

Another reason is that some jobs took longer than initially quoted: a job that should have taken 100 hours, took 130 and the price had already been given to the customers. Plus, there is some internal wastage, which is being addressed. We made some additional tweaks to get the company on track to more than double their profits this year. This just confirms how I have always described 80:20.

Are there lessons here for you? What might you discover if you split out your profit and loss by customer?

80:20 applies to every aspect of your business: customer profitability, product profitability, your marketing, sales people, office staff, etc.

The '*4-Hour Work Week*' Story

What is the best book title of all-time? I am not sure but '*The 4-Hour Work Week*' would certainly be on the short list. There is an interesting story about that title. The author, Tim Ferris, had a few different possible titles and was unsure which one to use, so he did an online survey and this title was the unanimous winner. But this is not the main story. The main story is about the author. Tim Ferris is a very famous author who has produced a whole series of '*4-Hour*' books ('*The 4-Hour Body*,' '*The 4-Hour Chef*' etc.). Though Tim was not always this successful.

Several years before, Tim had his own warehouse business but he was working eighty-hour weeks for an average wage (sound familiar?). He worked fifteen-hour days, six days every week. Then Tim discovered the 80:20 Principle and he conducted an analysis of his customers. He was astonished to find that of his 120 customers, just **five** of them accounted for 95% of his sales. He spend hours and days chasing 115 of his customers for just 5% of his sales.

He immediately changed the way he dealt with these 115 customers. Instead of him chasing these customers for orders, they had to fax them in. Instantly he saved hours and days of time. He put more time into his five good customers and secured extra orders from them. Within one month, Tim doubled his income and reduced his working week from eighty hours to fifteen. Not quite four hours but a significant reduction all the same. Tim embraced 80:20 in every aspect of his life.

Maximum income from minimum effort became his new mantra.

He wrote a book about these changes in his life which went on to be a bestseller (I am sure you can guess the title). To summarise Tim's change, he identified his most important tasks (selling to his top five customers) and did more of them. He knew his least important tasks (selling to those 115 customers who only gave him 5% of his sales) and cut hours and days off his tasks. 80:20 prioritisation is one of the keys to saving time and improving productivity.

80% of your customers give you 20% of your profit. While this sounds bad, it gets even worse because some of these 80% are actually losing you money.

80:20 Principle
A One-Woman Band

Just in case you think 80:20 only applies to manufacturing businesses or large organisations, I have an example below which shows that it applies to small businesses too.

These numbers are from a friend of mine, let us call her Mary, who works as a web designer. When I looked at her income per day, this is what it looked like...

Her average weekly income was around €1,000 and the daily split was as follows:

Monday, Tuesday, Wednesday & Friday her income was €50 per day, on Thursday her income was €800. The reason her income on Thursday was so much higher was because that company had a decent marketing budget. The other four days she did work for local businesses which had smaller budgets.

If she can find one other whale client with a budget like her Thursday one it will have a big effect on her income.

Then she would have two days at €800 and three days at €50, giving her a weekly income of €1,750. That is a 75% increase in income.

You may be looking at these numbers thinking it seems too good to be true or 'my business is different.' Think about your customers or products for a moment. Do you have customers you know give you a good profit for the time and effort that goes into them? At the other end of the scale are there customers or products where you think, 'For all the time and effort that goes in here, do I make any money?'

This is 80:20 at work, and if you ever sit down and do the numbers, they may be like the web designer above.

Know your best customers and know your worst ones. Replace the worst ones with good ones and watch your profit grow.

A Whale Is Worth 16 Times A Sardine

I know whales are very valuable but I have some numbers that will blow your mind.

Let us take a business with ten customers. 80:20 tells us that two of these customers are worth 80% to us and the other eight give us just 20%. Let us assume this company has sales of €100,000.

Whale clients are worth €80,000 so divided by two is €40,000 each (each whale client is worth €40,000 to us).

Sales to sardines are €20,000 so divide it by eight is €2,500 each (each sardine client is worth €2,500 to us).

Each whale is worth €40,000 while every sardine is worth €2,500.

That means a whale client is 16 times more valuable than a sardine (€40,000 divided by €2,500). Your best customer is worth 16 times your worst one.

That is amazing. What should you do with this information? Focus nearly all your attention on your best customers. Wrap them in cotton wool. Make sure they are happy. Buy these people lunch and find out how else you can serve them. This is good for them (extra service) and good for you (extra sales). Whatever sector they are in, go find more just like them. If they are a hotel, find more hotels.

Focus like a laser on looking after your current hotels and finding more like them. Then stand back and watch your bank balance grow.

Who said business was difficult?

> **Your most profitable customer is worth 16 times your least profitable.**
> **Just in case you had any doubt around 80:20, this should confirm its power to you.**

⚬⚬⚬

Strategy Number 1: Sell More To Your Whales

This is so easy. I was with a client when he told me this story. I think I would have loved this anyway but especially right now when I am so focused on 80:20.

Let us call him Michael. His sales increased this year by over 40%. That is a great achievement, especially in a very competitive sector. How did he do it? He identified his top customers and decided he wanted to increase sales with them.

- How did he approach this?
- Design new fancy products?
- Bring them to the top football games?
- Survey them?
- None of the above?

What did he do?

Michael went to his top customers and asked, "What do we have to do to grow our sales with you?"

Ok, he might not have been that blunt. But that is more or less what he did. And guess what? The customers told him.

It is a very competitive market so in some cases, he had to drop his price by 10c on an item selling for €6.50 (that is less than 2%). And by making a few changes like this they doubled their sales with their top customers. Which all helped his sales grow by over 40% this year.

A core message in 80:20 is:

'Your customers are not all the same, so do not treat them the same. Some are much more valuable than others. Know who they are and work closely to grow your sales with them. And focus your marketing on finding more like them.'

How difficult is that to do? Is there any reason why you cannot do this? The correct answer is, "No Neil, there is not." Is there any reason why you cannot do that this week? Ditto with the answer.

Just do it.

**Identify your most profitable clients (whales).
Sell more to them which will...
substantially increase your sales and profits.**

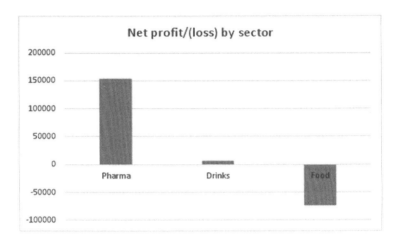

Graph 1

Strategy Number 2: Target Your Marketing At Finding More Whales

Once you have identified your whales and sardines, one of the biggest benefits to your business is that you can be much more selective about who you target as new customers. For example, if your whale customers are colleges, you can focus your marketing attention on finding new customers just like them.

I have worked with hundreds of businesses and the majority of them are guilty of two things. Firstly, they do not do a huge amount of marketing and when they do, it is a scattergun approach with no clear focus on who they want as a new customer.

When I ask business owners, 'Where do your customers come from or how do they find you?' most respond with, 'Word of mouth.'

80:20 changes all that. Armed with the knowledge of your most profitable customers, you can use laser focus to find more like them.

Example

Mike is a fabricator who supplied large manufacturing companies. When we completed his 80:20 analysis, we discovered something very interesting. A steel table was a very common product which he made for his customers. Everything was bespoke, which meant he designed and made it.

An average sale to a food customer was €4,000, while a similar table to a drinks company sold for €5,000. When he made a similar product for a pharmaceutical company, they paid €7,000. The material and labour for each of these tables was quite similar so his profit on the sale to the pharma customers was much bigger than to the other sectors. (See Graph 1). It seems each sector had a limit of what it would pay for these products. Pharma companies valued quality and reliability a bit more than the other sectors plus they had bigger budgets.

In the past, Mike had said yes to all business that came his way. When he realised that pharma jobs were much more profitable than other sectors, he put more time into finding others just like them. Within a few months, he added two more pharma customers to his existing one and his sales and profits increased accordingly. He found he was turning away smaller work from certain sectors.

Last time we spoke he was heading for a record year and had just booked his first, (what he called 'proper') family holiday in four years.

> **Like the before and after photos when people lose weight, 80:20 focuses you like a laser on finding new whale customers, which can take your profits to another level.**

Strategy Number 3: Develop Products For Your Best Customers

Mick is a marketing consultant who specialises in helping businesses grow their online sales. He is a big fan of email marketing and he has been sending daily emails to a list of 1,000 people for the last few years. These regular emails are conversational in tone, telling stories about funny events that happened to him and linking the story to a business tip. I take the same approach myself and it is a very effective way of communicating regularly with customers and prospects. It is a 'softly, softly' approach that enables the sender to communicate their expertise through entertaining stories.

Mick has built up a very loyal group of customers using this approach. Two years ago, he launched a 'members' club. Each member pays €37 per month and in return they receive a twelve-page newsletter with sales and marketing tips and a CD giving additional business advice. Although the monthly fee for this started out at €37, this steadily increased to the point where any new member now pays €150. This club brings in approximately €10,000 in sales every month. Running costs are relatively low, so he has a high profit level from this income. The members of this club include many of his A-type customers.

Mick has run many online training programmes which have been very successful. Through his open and honest communication with the group, he tells us that he knows in advance who will join these programs. Many of his A-type customers buy everything Mick produces. He calls them **hyper-responders**. His latest product is a **mastermind group**, where people pay €950 per month. He has twenty people signed up to this.

Mick's sales from this are €19,000 per month or €228,000 per year.

The feedback from the group is extremely good and I can see this mastermind group running for a long time.

How did he do this? How did he add over €350,000 in sales this year? Mick did this by focusing on his A-type customers, understanding their needs and developing products specifically for them.

How did he do this? He uses various methods to understand the needs of his top customers like surveys and the old-fashioned tactic of just asking them what they need.

> **We have all heard that it is '6 times easier to sell to an existing client.' The 80:20 take on that is, 'It is so much easier to sell more high-end services to your whale clients.'**

17

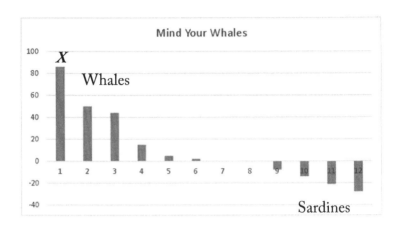

Graph 2

Strategy Number 4: Mind Your Customers

In the first part of this book, I told you the story of the electronics company and how my life changed forever when I stumbled on 80:20 and realised that just three of their thirty-six customers were giving them 91% of their net profits. One of these three whale customers accounted for the bulk of this profit at 60%.

I am now going to tell you a story about a company I worked for who did not mind their biggest whale company (X). (See Graph 2 above).

Now this most profitable customer (X) was growing rapidly. And X was looking for greater levels of customer service, but the company had always allocated support resources evenly across products. The most profitable customer got the same support levels as one who lost them money. This was a crazy situation.

I spoke to management urging them to allocate more resources to X, their super whale customer. They did not want to upset their D-type customers, who lost them money, so they left things as they were. And the inevitable happened. Shortly afterwards X, their whale customer left. They were not happy with the level of customer service they had received. This was so frustrating as it was preventable.

This 80:20 principle applies to every business. That means yours too.

Not all your customers are worth the same to you. Some are much more profitable than others.

And though it might not be nice to dwell on this too long, some of your customers are losing you money. Take the time and trouble to find out who your most valuable customers are. Look after them well. Call into them. Thank them for their business. Make sure they have no issues with your business. These customers are like gold dust, so look after them.

> **Not all customers are the same. Some are much more valuable than others. These whale customers are like gold dust.**
> **Know who they are and look after them very well.**

———

Was This Fair?

John arrives at Heathrow Airport around 3pm. A flight is due to leave from London to Paris at 4pm. However, John is not booked on the flight, it is fully booked and there is a stand-by list with forty-one people ahead of him. His chances do not look very good, do they?

In the end, there was just one seat on the plane and John got it.

How did this happen? It happened for one reason only. John had a few million air miles and flew with the airline on a regular basis over many years. He was a Gold customer and the airline saw him as more valuable than the other passengers.

Does this seem fair? Probably not. The airline looked at the forty-two people on their stand-by list and choose the person they saw as most valuable to them. John had spent over €20,000 with the airline in recent years compared to the other passengers who had spent a few hundred.

As a business owner, how does this affect you? Well, you have a mix of customers and that most likely means a small number of John-types who spend lots with you and a large group of other passenger-types who spend small amounts. Do you treat all these customers the same? You may think this is the right way to treat your customers and it is your business, so you are 100% entitled to do this.

As long as you are aware that treating all customers the same is costing you money and profits.

If you are like most business owners I know, you work long hours and finding time for things like talking to customers or surveying them is difficult. Doing the everyday work of the business takes most of your time, leaving little left for marketing and other similar activities.

I bet you have a list of things you would like to do – talk with customers more, drop in if you are passing by or phone and arrange to meet for a coffee. How much time have you spent on those activities in the last year? Despite the best will in the world, I would think the answer to that question is 'very little.'

Here is the simple truth of business: we simply do not have a lot of time to look after every customer and talk with them as we would like to. If you have 100 customers, you certainly do not have time for this. But what if you knew your top 20 customers, could you find time to talk with them?

> **Your whale customers are more important than your sardine ones. Do not try to feed a whale customer the same amount of resources as a sardine.**

Strategy Number 5: Fire Your Sardines!

Mrs Murphy was very excited. Her grandson's twenty-first birthday was in four weeks' time and she promised to help organise the big party. She called to Mick the printer to get the invitations. Her father had always dealt with Mick's father so she would never dream of going anywhere else.

This was a big deal for Mrs Murphy; she wanted to make sure everything was perfect. She sat down with the printer for thirty minutes going through different colours and designs. She could not make up her mind and took some different designs home to show her daughter. She returned the next day with one selected. She wanted to see a draft of the invitation before printing started.

She called back two days later, inspected the design and insisted on two more changes. The printer finalised the design. Then he set up the printer, changing colours and settings according to her specifications. He ran one hundred invitations through and inspected the first few. There was a slight smudge on the edge and knowing how fussy Mrs. Murphy would be, he decided to run them through again. This time they came out perfect. He sent them through to the next workstation for cutting and packaging. From here the invitations were sent to accounts and an invoice was raised. Mrs. Murphy received a phone call saying her invitations were ready for collection. She looked at the invites and was delighted with how they turned out. She had no money on her but promised to drop a cheque up the following week and off she went.

Mrs Murphy was charged just €70 for this job. Mrs. Murphy's invitations should have been invoiced at over €200 but they were not. Why? Because she would never pay that, so the business was losing money on her order. There is a minimum cost of dealing with every customer and in Mrs Murphy's case this was €200.

Do you know the minimum cost of dealing with a customer in your business and how many of your customers are being charged less than this amount?

How do I know about all these steps? Because I tracked a sample of jobs for the printer. He is a client of mine and I knew from going in there, that just like most other businesses, he had a mix of different clients. I tracked a selection of jobs and costed them. They had other customers like colleges and hospitals who placed big repeat orders and were very profitable. I term these big profitable customers 'whales', while the likes of Mrs Murphy are 'sardines' who lose you money, are awkward to deal with and slow to pay.

Mrs. Murphy's law? It is otherwise known as the Pareto law or Pareto principle, aka the 80:20 Principle. And it applies to every business – including yours.

> **There is always a minimum cost of taking on a customer. Many business owners are so focused on sales, they do not think about profitability.**

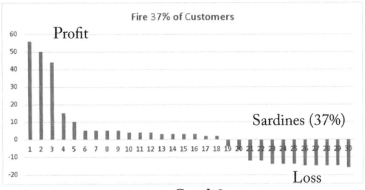

Graph 3

Fire 37% Of Your Customers

She did not hold back. "Neil, have you lost your mind? Fire customers – fire 37% of my customers!! Are you insane?" Her reaction was both expected and not unusual. But unfortunately for Sharon, the numbers do not lie. I had just completed my 80:20 analysis of her accounts and worked out the net profit/net loss per customer. And the bad news for Sharon was that 37% of her customers were losing her money. (See Graph 3 above). How is this possible?

Surely all customers are good, right?

Sharon owns a business making blinds and curtains. While the 80:20 analysis showed that 37% of customers lose her money was a huge surprise to her, unfortunately it was less so for me, as I have seen this trend many times over the last twenty years.

Like many businesses, Sharon has a mix of customers, some of whom spend thousands while others spend hundreds. And it is the smaller customer orders which cause the problems, as there is a minimum amount of time and effort which must go into each one. I tracked several customer orders through the system. The sale is an eleven-step process:

1) A prospect emails or phones with an enquiry and an appointment is booked for a sales rep to call to the house.

2) The rep visits the house, measures the windows and takes the customer details. This quotation information is brought back to the administration department.

3) If the prospect has not placed an order within one week, the rep follows up with a phone call to try to secure the order.

4) The customer places the order, pays 50% deposit and administration key in the order details and email it to the supplier.

5) The order arrives and the delivery is checked against purchase order details to ensure it is correct. Unfortunately, 20% of the time, the order is incorrect. Then the supplier must be contacted to send the correct materials.

6) Administration contact the customer to arrange a fitting date. Before the fitting date, the correct blinds are checked and prepared for the fitter.

7) Occasionally the customer cancels at the last moment and fittings must be rearranged.

8) The fitter calls to the house, collects final payment, fits the blinds, finalises the paperwork and returns it to administration.

9) Administration process the paperwork and payment.

10) The sales order is processed by administration along with the supplier invoices.

11) Customers can also call to the showroom and a sales assistant could spend fifteen minutes going through various options, for a sale of €100.

All these steps must be followed whether the order is for €100 or €1,000. Many of Sharon's orders are €200 or less. While the gross margin is around 53%, each order consumes overhead costs like rep salaries, transport costs, administration costs and fitters' wages. Gross Margin is the difference between selling price and the cost of materials so if she had a sale of €200 and the material cost was €90, the gross profit would be €110, €200 - €90 = €110. This is often expressed as a percentage of gross profit divided by selling price or €110 divided by €200 = 55%.

On top of this, a portion of all overheads must also be allocated to customers, as this is the only way these costs can be recouped. An allocation of overheads must be made to each order for rent and rates, insurance, phones, marketing, accountancy, stationery, etc. Without even getting into the numbers it is easy to see how orders of less than €200 will lose money.

As we saw in the earlier example with Mrs Murphy, there is a minimum cost of doing business with any customer – remember not all customers are the same.

Most business owners do not realise or appreciate just how high this figure can get. While most pricing and costing systems can work for larger orders or medium-size ones, they do not adequately cover the costs involved with smaller customer orders. This is how Sharon is losing money on 37% of customers. So what are her options for dealing with these customers?

She could:

1. Increase selling prices.
2. Reduce the level of service.
3. Try to sell more higher value orders to loss making sardine customers.
4. Send them to her competitors.

From my experience, the main option is number one and while some customers will still stay, many will move to a competitor's business. This is often the source of much amusement for my clients as their competitors welcome these loss-makers with open arms, not realising that they will probably lose money on these small value orders.

How applicable is all this to your business? I would be very surprised if something similar does not apply to your business. How do I know this? Because 80:20 is a natural law, just like gravity, so you cannot really escape it. I suggest you crunch some numbers and work out the cost of dealing with smaller customers. And just like Sharon and many more, you may have to put up your prices and say goodbye to many of these loss-makers.

> **With customers who lose you money (sardines), you must increase your prices. This will either move them up or out.**

How Firing Customers Helps Profits

In an earlier section I told the story of Mrs Murphy and the printer. She struck a chord with many people. To recap the story of her and my printer client, Mrs Murphy took up loads of time, was only charged €70 for the job, so he lost money on her and she was slow to pay. Does this sound familiar? Do you have customers like Mrs Murphy?

At the other end of the scale, the printer has customers like colleges who place big repeat orders, are profitable and pay on time. This should sound familiar to you and you should hopefully have good profitable customers.

At this stage, I have advised hundreds of businesses and this scenario applies in every single one of them. Businesses have a mix of good customers and not so good customers. That in itself would not be critical if the mix was in favour of the profitable customers but unfortunately, it is not. This is where 80:20 comes into play.

If the printer had one hundred customers, roughly twenty of them would be like the college and eighty like Mrs Murphy. I am not saying the 80:20 applies exactly in every case. I have seen it as high as 90:10, and also seen it at 70:30.

The important message here is that, **a small number of your customers account for a large percentage of your sales and profits, and, a large number of customers account for a small percentage of your sales and profits.** How does this happen? It happens because of the **80:20 Principle**. 80:20 is a naturally occurring law.

Look at the wealth distribution in the world. Look at how often we wear a small number of our clothes while most stuff in our wardrobe is rarely worn. 80:20 is everywhere and it's a naturally occurring law.

Firing customers seems alien to business owners. But once you know customers like Mrs Murphy are losing you money, you have two choices: increase her prices or fire her, (send her to your competition).

You may be asking, 'Why fire her?' Because she is taking up time and resources that could be better spent on a more profitable customer. At the same time, you could be selling more to your profitable customers and focusing all your marketing efforts on finding more like them. You may be sceptical about this. You may be thinking, **'But my business is different.' These are the five most dangerous words in business.** Unless you have crunched the numbers and worked out your customer profitability, you cannot say for sure if 80:20 applies to your business.

Critical Step Before Firing A Customer

When working with a client on 80:20, the fun starts when you identify your whales and sardines. Sardines are often small customers and if I mention increasing prices or firing them, I often get this response: 'What if a current small customer becomes a big one in the future?' This is a very valid question and one I am often asked.

We address this in the classification of your customers. The first step is to split profit and loss by customer, so we often have a small number of very profitable customers (whales) and lots of loss-makers (sardines). With one recent client, we had three whales and eleven sardines. With another, we had seven whales and forty-three sardines. The trend is always similar – it is only the numbers that differ. No doubt, your business is the same with a small number of whales and lots of sardines.

Before I finalise my classification, I go through another few steps and I introduce a new category – that of **baby whale**. You may well ask, what is a **baby whale**? This is a small customer now, who is losing you money but has the potential to be a whale. Think back to Mrs Murphy, a grandmother, who bought from my printer client once every few years. Whale clients for the printer are hospitals and colleges. How likely was it that Mrs Murphy would ever become a **baby whale**? Highly unlikely, I would think. However, they had a college who was a small customer but with similar characteristics to the whales. I would classify this as a 'baby whale' and move them across to my A-type category.

The message here is clear.

> **Your business has whales (very profitable customers), sardines (loss makers) and baby whales (loss makers now but with the potential to be a whale in the near future). Your whales and baby whales are much more important than your sardines.**

Business Lessons From Starbucks

If you sell a product for €100, then you should also have one for €500 and €5,000. Why? Because a small number of people are willing to spend those amounts of money.

How do I know? It comes from something called the Power Curve and it was developed by Perry Marshall. I cannot get enough of Perry's books and writing. He has taken the 80:20 Principle and added some layers to it, and one of those is his Power Curve model. This model can be used to predict with reasonable accuracy how much people will spend for a product.

Here is an example:

One hundred customers have paid €100 for a product. His model predicts that twenty of them are willing to spend €400 with your company. Four of them are willing to spend €1,600. And one of them would spend €5,000.

This has been tested on hundreds of businesses.

Let us take Starbucks as an example. Say somebody goes to Starbucks and spends €4 on a coffee. According to the model, somebody is willing to spend €300 in Starbucks but how can they do that? They could buy an Espresso machine for €300. Starbucks show they understand the Power Curve model by making these products available and some people do buy them. They maximise their sales by doing so.

Large football stadiums like Croke Park in Dublin is another good example. You can get as terrace ticket for €20, a stand one for €80 or you can buy a corporate box for €250,000 for the year. These corporate boxes are massively profitable and a key part of new stadiums everywhere. The old Croke Park stadium had no corporate boxes and was missing out on a large income stream.

And the same applies to your business. You need to provide a range of products and services so that a certain percentage of people can give you more money. Firstly consider what is your average sale?

If it is €50 then that means that one in every five customers is willing to spend €200 with you. But you must have the product available for them. And you must encourage those people to spend more with you. Otherwise you are leaving a lot of money on the table.

> **One in five customers is willing to spend four times more with you. If your average sale is €200 and you have 100 customers, then 20 of them are willing to spend €800 with you, for a superior version of the same product. Having this option could almost double your sales.**

Perry's Power Curve

I have been reading some new 'stuff' and thought I would share some of it with you. I have become an even bigger fan of 80:20 as I have been studying some ideas from Perry Marshall. Perry has taken 80:20 and come up with some revolutionary ideas on how you can use it to take your profits onto another planet. This stuff could blow your mind, so I had better start with one that will only double your sales.

20% of your customers are willing to spend five times more than they are spending with you right now. Now this is not just theory but has been proven in lots of different businesses across the globe. There are other numbers around this principle but I am going to stick with this one for now.

Example

A business has 100 customers and each one spends, on average, €1,000 over a year. Some will spend more and others will spend less but their average spend is €1,000 each. The principle says that, 20% of your customers are willing to spend five times more than they are spending with you right now; in this case that would mean twenty customers are willing to spend €5,000 per year. 20 x €5,000 = €100,000. This business can double their sales if they can identify this 20%. In case you are sceptical about this, I know of at least two businesses that have taken this approach and their profits have more than doubled. Do you think this can be done in your business?

How To Work Out the 80:20 For Your Business

The first step involves number crunching and while I realise finances are not everybody's favourite topic, in this case, there is no avoiding them. You will need either a full set of twelve-month accounts or accounts for a three to six-month period. You will need a profit and loss account, plus analysis of sales.

You can use a sheet of paper but an excel spreadsheet is preferable.

1. Product/Customer: Along the top of the sheet you can list your main products or customers. You will have to decide yourself which one is most relevant to your business.

2. Sales: You want to split your sales figures across the sheet by customer, so the total at the end agrees with the total sales figure from your profit and loss.

3. Suppliers: If you own a product business which has suppliers, then you need to allocate their costs by customer.

4. Salaries/Wages: Salaries and wages are usually a big cost for most businesses, so you should allocate these to customers.

5. Overheads: These are all your other costs excluding supplier and payroll. Some of these costs may be relatively easy to allocate to customers. With other costs, like rent or administration staff, it is more difficult. All you can do with these costs is fix some way of allocating them to customers, i.e. % of sales.

At the end of this exercise, your total sales and total costs should be allocated across all customers. At the bottom of the spreadsheet, you will see which customers are profitable and which are losing you money.

I normally distinguish customer categories as follows:

A-type = most profitable customers

B-type = small profit

C-type = break-even

D-type = losing you money

Plan Of Action

1. A-type customers are like gold dust and you need to mind them, so you should meet with and survey your most profitable customers to see if there are any issues with your products and services.

2. Sell more of your current products to your A-type customers.

3. Revise your sales and marketing plan so you focus most of the efforts on finding more A-type customers.

4. Survey the most profitable customers, identify their needs and develop new products specifically with them in mind.

5. With D-type customers, you must reduce your costs and/or increase prices. This will move them up to a B-type customer or else they will move on to buy from a competitor.

SECTION 2 SELLING PRICE

MAXIMISE PROFITS THROUGH YOUR PRICES

The Antique Jewellery Story

This story was taken from the fabulous book, *'Persuasion'* by Robert Cialdini.

Some years ago, a woman owned and ran a jewellery shop. She invested in a range of antique jewellery and placed it in the front window. It sat there for a long time and not one item sold. She was getting sick of looking at this jewellery. She was about to go on holidays and decided she wanted this antique range gone by the time she got back. She scribbled a note to her manager 'Adjust price by half!' and off she went.

When she returned two weeks later, she was relieved to see all the jewellery gone. She thought to herself, 'I made no money on it but at least it is gone.'

The following Monday she sat down with her manager to go through the figures. She was pleasantly surprised to find the sales figures were higher than she expected – even with the half price jewellery. When she expressed her surprise at the higher sales to the manager, she responded, "Yes, it was amazing how quickly the antique jewellery sold when we doubled the price."

"Doubled the price?" the owner exclaimed. "My note said to half the price."

And it was at that very moment it dawned on both owner and manager what had happened.

The scribbled note of 'adjust by half' had been misinterpreted by the manager as 'adjust by two' and she had doubled the price. A piece that had not sold at €40, now sold out at €80.

What conclusions can we draw from this story?

Why did the jewellery suddenly sell when the price doubled?

There really is only one conclusion we can make…

People's perceptions about the jewellery were:

Lower price = lower quality

Higher price = higher quality

What lessons are here for you on pricing? What does this mean when the next person haggles with you over price? The price you choose for your product or service is making a statement about its perceived quality, not its real quality (as price will not change that) but its perceived quality.

Next time you pick a low price as you think, 'nobody will pay that' or 'that is too expensive,' you will be making a statement about your product.

Why not make a bold statement on price? People will perceive it as higher quality. I am not saying everybody will be happy to pay the higher price as you will still encounter price conscious shoppers. You just need to ensure you find the quality focused shoppers, just like at the jewellery shop.

People's perceptions are like this
Lower price = lower quality
Higher price = higher quality
What do people think when they hear your prices?

Lessons from Four Older Women

I was working with a woman who owned a café. Although the café was very busy, this woman had not paid herself a wage for over a year. Her profit margins were too low. She needed to make some changes and one of those was to put up her prices. She fought hard against it.

She gave the example of four women who came in every morning after mass, for their coffee and scone. She was sure they would notice. She finally relented and put up her prices 10%. The only people who noticed were the four mass women, who took their business elsewhere. She kept all her other customers.

Because the additional sales from her price increase is pure profit, she had enough extra money in the till at the end of the week to pay herself a wage.

I met her two weeks later and she said, "You will not believe what happened – the four women came back." They had taken their business elsewhere but had found the scones were not as nice and the place was not as welcoming so they returned.

Price is not the only factor in buying decisions.

> **Studies show price is only the main factor in 15% of buying decisions. As illustrated by these 4 women and their café, price is not the only factor when your customers are making a buying decision.**

Do You Always Buy the Cheapest?

There was a very interesting discussion on our forum. It was started by a roofing contractor. Let us call him Michael. The gist of his email was something like this:

"Everybody is looking for the cheapest price. My competition is undercutting me and getting the jobs – even though their work is not up to scratch. I have cut my prices and do not want to reduce them anymore. I am well established and do a high-quality job. How can I get more jobs without having to cut prices further?"

Does this sound familiar to you? This is a story I have heard from numerous clients, especially in recent years.

I asked Michael if he always buys the cheapest goods. For example, if he is shopping for work boots, does he buy the cheapest?

He replied, that he went for quality as he knew these would last longer.

"Does the same logic not apply to your customers?" I asked him. Then I asked him about Lidl, the discount grocery chain. Since the recession, it seems many people have switched from the large supermarket chains to the 'cheaper' shops like Lidl. And yet they only have 13% of the Irish grocery market. That means every week 87% of people are choosing to shop for their groceries in the bigger, more expensive supermarkets. Why is this? The only logical answer is that price is not the only consideration when people are deciding where to buy.

Other factors are taken into consideration:

- **Price is often not the number one factor when somebody is buying from you.**
- **Other factors like quality, convenience, brand and reputation are also important.**

To me, there are a number of different aspects to Michael's story. One is Michael's own *mindset* and beliefs about his work and how to price it. Another is *positioning*. What message is he giving out to potential customers? And *marketing* is another. I would guess if he is competing on price with his competition, that his potential customers are finding him.

Pricing, positioning and marketing are all interconnected. Do any of these sound familiar to you? There are a number of different approaches to counter this problem.

One approach would be for Michael to have a consumer guide '5 Things to Look for In Your New Roof.' This will give the prospective customer useful information and position Michael as an expert in this area.

Do you have hassle from customers looking for discounts? Do you always buy the cheapest? Price is not the only factor.
Only 15% of time is price the main factor.

The €100 Nail

'That is very expensive!' or 'You will have to sharpen your pencil there.' These must be two of the most common responses business people hear when they mention price to customers. Have you heard them from your customers? I have often had conversations with clients about people haggling over price. And this story came to mind. Even if you have heard it before, it is worth hearing again.

A woman had a squeak on her hallway floor for years. Numerous tradesmen had come to look at it but none were able to fix it. Then somebody told her of a man who could fix her squeak for good. The man called to the house and spent a few minutes walking around her hallway. Then he walked to a spot and hammered a nail into the floor. He asked the woman to walk across her hallway. She walked across and was amazed to find her squeak was gone.

She was overjoyed. Overjoyed that is until the man told her his bill was €100.

"But you were only here for a few minutes," she said. "How can it be €100?" The man took out a pen and paper, wrote for a minute and handed the paper to the woman.

It read: *Nail €2. Knowing where to put the nail €98. Total €100.*

The moral of this story is that **knowledge carries a value**. Knowledge that can help people has a value. Seeing how many business people approach pricing, I could envision a few people only charging this woman €10 or €20 for this job. They would think like the woman did, 'Ah sure it is only a few minutes. I cannot charge the woman more than €20.'

> **In business, you need to be more like the tradesman and value what you do. Reflect the value of what you do in your selling price.**

Pricing Lessons from Picasso

A woman was walking down a street in Paris and she was amazed to see Picasso sketching at the side of the street. She knew that he does not usually sketch people but still asked him and was pleasantly surprised when he agreed. A short while later, he handed the woman her sketch and when she asked, "How much do I owe you?" he replied, "5,000 Francs". The woman was shocked at the price and said to the painter, "But it only took you a few minutes, how can it be 5,000 Francs?" The famous painter replied, "No, my dear, that took me a whole lifetime."

> **Like Picasso, your knowledge and experience have taken a long time to accumulate. Ensure this valuable knowledge is reflected in your prices.**

Put Your Prices Up 10%

I run marketing/selling training courses on a regular basis. I must admit, I do love training. A lot of it is more facilitation as I throw out a topic and let a group of ten or twelve business owners discuss it and share ideas.

I had a recent group and did a little bit of role play. I addressed the group. "Let us suppose for a moment that I am going to give you all an instruction and you must go into your business tomorrow morning and implement it. Is that ok with everyone?" I ask. I see nods of approval around the room.

"Ok, I want you to go into your business tomorrow morning and increase all your selling prices by 10%." Looks of puzzlement flashed across the faces around the room.

"Well, are you all ok with doing that first thing tomorrow morning?" I asked. They are not amused and the comments start coming.

"No."

"Cannot do that."

"Why not?" I asked. "I would lose all my customers!" one responded.

"Why do your customers buy from you and not somebody else?" I asked. "Are they only buying from you on price?" "No," chorused the group.

"Give me some other reasons they buy from you?" I asked.

"I have an agency for my product and it is the best in the market," said the parts supplier. "My clients know if they have an issue, even on a Sunday morning, that I will have somebody there to sort it out," replied the flooring guy.

"Ok, we have established that your customers are buying from you for reasons other than price. That is good." I said. "Are you the cheapest in your market?" "No," said the group. "Are you the dearest?" I asked, "No," they said.

"Why are you not the dearest?" I asked. "Is the most expensive guy better than you?"

Obviously, I am not telling them to go increase their prices the next day.

The purpose of the exercise is to make them think about their selling price and the attitude towards it.

Ditto to you as a business owner. I see lots of people get their selling price wrong and it is never set too high but often put too low. Which can result in low profits and cash flow problems. How do you set your selling price? Look at your competitors and set it a bit lower?

Do you ever drop your prices because you think your customers will not pay a higher price even though they have not asked you to drop your prices?

Plus, you will always get hagglers over price, so do not let them stop you setting the right selling price for your business. Get this one wrong and your business will always struggle. I have worked with hundreds of businesses and many of them get their selling price wrong. I rarely have to tell them to drop it, as more often than not, it is set too low. As in the example above, fear is a big factor.

I encourage almost everybody I work with to increase their selling prices as nothing has a bigger impact on profits. In many cases prices have not increased for years and cost are always going up so they need to be increased to cover this.

Why You Should Never Discount

I received a phone call from a friend one Friday. She supplies uniforms to hotels. She had a potential new customer who was pushing hard for a discount. She was asking me if she should give it. Now in this situation many people give a discount because they believe that otherwise the sales might be lost. Especially in the last few years with downward pressure on prices, the temptation is even greater to give a discount.

Each business owner must decide for themselves what to do in this situation. Back to my friend in Dublin. Now I do not know her profit margins but I went through some numbers with her. Imagine for a moment that these are the numbers for a typical business..

Total Sales €100

Total costs €80

Profit €20

Believe me, I am being generous here because the profit element is even smaller for most businesses but let us go with these numbers for now.

Now if she gives a 10% discount her numbers will be:
Total sales €90
Total costs €80
Profit €10

The selling price will drop from €100 to €90, her costs stay at €80, her profit will drop from €20 to €10. That is a 50% drop in her profits.

Many people do not realise this but any change to your selling price goes straight to the bottom line. Or to put it another way, if she gives everybody a 10% discount, she will have to find double the number of customers to achieve the same profit. Conversely if she increased her prices by 10% her numbers would change to:
Total Sales €110
Total costs €80
Profit €30

Her profit would increase from €20 to €30, that is a 50% increase in profits. Now many people would say that you cannot put up your prices in the current climate but I have worked with two businesses who have increased their prices in the current climate with no adverse effect.

Rather than give a discount, try to give the customer something extra that they will put a high value on but has a small cost to you. One furniture shop I worked with gave extras, like cushions or candles, free and the customer was delighted – even though their purchase may have been in the region of €2,000.

> **A business with a 20% profit margin, giving a 10% discount, reduces its profit by 50%. You would need double the number of customers to stay still, profit wise.**

Are Your Selling Prices Set Correctly?

I had a coffee with a guy who had recently started his business. He specialises in social media and I have heard he is very good; one of the best around in his speciality. The conversation covered marketing, networking and selling price. The conversation on selling price went something like this.

"How do you price your jobs?" I asked Jim.

"I estimate the time by my hourly rate." Jim replied.

"How did you arrive at the hourly rate?" I asked.

"It is based on my income target per month," said Jim. "Ok, that sounds good." I nodded at him.

"People tell me you are very good at what you do. Tell me, how do your hourly rates compare with your competition?" I asked him.

"Mine are about half their rate." Jim said. "Half their rate – why is it half their rate? Is your work inferior to theirs?" I said incredulous.

"No, it is every bit as good," he replied.

"Then why are you only charging half the rate?" I asked Jim.

At this point, Jim came out with the line I have heard one hundred times or more (a bit like the song).

"Well, they charge X and are in business a long time and as

I am only starting, I decided to charge half their rate."

Even though I have heard this numerous times and can understand why people say this, it still makes no sense to me. It completely ignores the customer and the value they get from the work. I continued chatting to Jim and am quite confident that he will be increasing his prices soon.

This will have a big impact on his business as all those extra sales will be 100% profit.

Many businesses I work with have set their selling price incorrectly and this has a major negative effect on their profits and cash flow.

And guess how many set it too high? Yes – none.

It is always set too low. So, there is a good chance that your selling price is set wrongly too and that it is set too low. This too can have a huge negative effect on your profits and cash flow.

> **Many start-ups set their prices by looking at their competition and picking a lower figure. There is a good reason why the competition is higher than them, so do not fall into that trap.**

SECTION 3

MARKETING EFFECTIVELY WITH NO MONEY

Do You Have Constipation?

Do not worry, I have not lost the plot here.

This is the headline of a flyer I got in my door recently. I kept it because it was such a great example of a marketing piece. Just yesterday I received another flyer and I was looking at it for a few seconds to figure out what they were selling. Many marketing pieces are badly designed. People, by nature, are scanners. We spend just two or three seconds scanning anything to find out if we want to read further.

Just think about reading a newspaper. We scan the pages looking at headlines or pictures to see if we want to read further. Studies have been conducted to find out how long people spend reading a newspaper. On average, they spend just four seconds on each page.

Why Am I Telling You All This?

- Because there are rules to be followed when designing any marketing piece.
- Because people have such short attention spans, these rules are designed to grab the attention of people who may be interested in your product.

If you are going to run an ad, email campaign, flyer, brochure or even a website, you need to know these rules.

The 'Constipation' flyer is a good example of how it should be done.

Do you have constipation? (good headline).

Are you over 18 and would you like... (clearly defining their market).

Reimbursement for travel... (an offer/incentive to respond to).
Phone... or email... (a clear call to action).

These are the rules you should follow in running any marketing piece/flyer, etc.

- Business people think their ad must appeal to everybody. Wrong. The headline must only appeal to your target market.
- Let us say 5% of the population suffer from constipation. The headline is designed to appeal only to them. They do not care if the other 95% of the population throw it in the bin.
- The offer and call to action are also critical in any marketing literature.

Keep these rules close at hand the next time you are running any marketing.

The rules of marketing are similar regardless of what you are doing.
Good headline (Do you have constipation?)
Clearly defined market (Are you over 18?)
Reimbursement (Offer)
Phone or e-mail (Call to Action)

Bloodless Marketing

As business owners, we sometimes put ourselves through blood, sweat and tears marketing our business; would it not be great if we found a painless (bloodless) marketing strategy?

It is not every day I walk into a client and get greeted by a big sloppy kiss. Well, it was more like a big sloppy licking really. Before you get overly excited, I had just started working with a new client who happened to be a vet and the greeting came from Jessie, a large affectionate Labrador.

I must admit I am a dog-lover, so I did not mind being assaulted with all this affection. What was more remarkable about the greeting was that Jessie had been under the knife just an hour earlier. John has the latest high spec keyhole surgery equipment which is painless for the animals and hence his saying 'bloodless surgery.'

Well, a little bit further on in the meeting, we stumbled on one but not before we discussed many different ideas for their business. Then John's wife Mary, almost as an aside, mentioned a promotion they ran the previous year which resulted in fifty new customers. My ears immediately perked up. I asked Mary to tell me a bit more about the campaign. They had run a promotion through another company that offered a discount on vaccinations but when customers came in they still bought extra things – making the offer a big success. But to me the real success is in the lifetime value of these new clients. If the average dog lives twelve years, how many trips will they make to the vet?

To me the big lesson in this is that they did something which worked well and then stopped and never ran it again.

Why would you stop when you find something that worked well? We have all done it and I am as guilty as anybody but have you done something in your business that worked very well and then you stopped or forgot about it?
What idea worked well the last time, that can you try again?

What sales or marketing worked very well before?
When you find marketing that works, keep doing it.

Rocky and the Squirrel

I took Rocky, my sister's dog, for a walk earlier in the week; himself and the rabbits are almost on speaking terms. He makes a token effort to chase them and they pretend to run away a little bit. I think they do it out of sympathy just to satisfy his dog ego.

He has never quite grasped the 'dog chasing rabbit' bit of being a dog. I think he was missing from dog school the day that was done...The O'Brien dogs of previous generations would disown him.

Anyway, we were out for our walk and suddenly Rocky got excited and chased after something. My hopes were raised. Maybe he was finally coping on to the idea of chasing a rabbit. But when I took a closer look I discovered he was chasing a... squirrel. Now I know his eyesight is not the best but... a squirrel and a rabbit. Dogs chase rabbits not squirrels. **Not his target market.**

> **Is it possible you are making the same mistake in business? Wasting time chasing after people who are not your target market.**

Lesson 101 in marketing – not everybody is your target market! Yet many people I talk to in business never sit down and decide their target market.

Why do you need to do this? Because not everybody is the right fit for your business. Time and money can be wasted chasing after the 'wrong' market.

I spoke a man this week who spent an hour talking to a woman about a new kitchen.

His minimum kitchen is €15,000.

Her budget was €5,000.

Meeting over. Now that hour could have been spent on more productive activities.

By asking a few qualifying questions right at the start, you can filter people in or out of your sales process. Believe me I know this as I have wasted time in the past talking to people who were not my target market.

How will you know your target market? You can start by looking at your current customers. Better still, narrow it down and look at your best customers. And get more like them. Know your target market, the people most likely to buy from you.

> **How well do you know your target market? If you are not clear look at people who bought from you before. Do not be like Rocky chasing squirrels instead of rabbits. Know your target market and focus on these people.**

No Mushrooms Allowed

In town, I was killing time between client meetings. I wandered into a book store and a book title grabbed my eye, '*No Mushrooms Allowed*.' And I thought, 'what a brilliant title for a book. And what a great marketing lesson.'

I was running some training courses at that time and I brought the book into one group for discussion. I do not know the figures, but let us say 5% of the population do not like mushrooms. 95% do and will never be interested in buying this book.

But that is fine as the other 5% will be very interested. That is their niche – people who do not like mushrooms.

In business, you too need to know your niche and target market.

When I ask business owners the question, "Who is your target market?" most respond with "Everybody!"

And of course, they are wrong because your target market is not everybody.

As a coincidence, when discussing email marketing with this particular group, one woman told us how she had received an email from somebody selling scarves the previous day and she had bought one. Now if that email came to me, I would not have bought one. I am not their target market, whereas she was.

Had I received an email selling golf clubs or hill-walking gear, then I may be interested, but you may not be. And that is one of the keys steps you must get right to grow your sales. You need to be aiming your marketing message at your target market. Your message must arrive at people who have an interest in what you sell.

There is no point trying to sell bibles to Atheists. Or selling pork sausages to vegetarians.

How Will You Know Your Target Market?

Just look at people who bought from you before. Better still, in true 80:20 style, aim your message at your juiciest market. Those most profitable customers (whales). Aim your marketing message at them and people like them. Keep that mushroom book in mind when planning your marketing. Remember, you do not need to target everyone, just your own most likely to buy, non-mushroom loving people.

> **Just like everybody does not like mushrooms, not everybody is your target market. A person selling a recipe book that has no mushrooms, wants to get their message in front of people who do not eat mushrooms. Likewise, you want to get your message in front of your target market.**

Would You Bring This Man Home to Your Mother?

Singles ad 1

Guy, 36, likes going to the local with friends and watching telly. No strong preference on location as can travel. Have an open mind on age.

Singles ad 2

30-year-old woman would like to meet a guy aged between 30-35 in the Cork area. Interests are keeping fit, going to the gym a few times a week and also loves hill-walking and outdoor activities. Friends and family are very important to her. Must like dogs as she has two. Non-smoker essential.

Of the two, which one is more likely to be successful? Which one has a clear idea of themselves and what they want?

I am sure to most people, it is obvious that the woman has a very clear idea of what she likes and the type of man that she would like to meet. The guy is a bit vague on what he is about and very general in terms of what he is looking for.

For business owners, there are very clear lessons in these two ads on how we approach business. There are also important parallels on our approach to marketing. Many business people I encounter are like this guy – not very clear on what they do and if I ask them who their target market is they say 'everybody.'

Saying that your target market is everybody is a big mistake I hear from business people all the time and shows how little they understand their marketing.

They would be well advised to look at the woman's ad above and take some lessons from it.

Is she likely to be interested in the couch potato above who spends his weekend in the pub? No, because she has clearly stated her preference in terms of age, location and interests.

Is she likely to go to the pub to meet her ideal man? No, she is more likely to go to the gym or join a hill-walking club as she knows that where her target market will be.

> **In business, we need to be very clear on what we do, especially our USP (like the woman above).**
> **Then we need to get equally clear on our target market and our ideal customer (unlike the man in the ad above).**

Dating in the Digital Age

Some Sundays, rather than going to the gym, I treat myself to the steam room and sauna. Last Sunday when I went into the steam room, there were two guys there in their mid-20s. I sat down and these guys were chatting away. At first, I thought they were speaking some foreign language and then I realised they were two local lads, with very strong Cork accents. Between their accents and lingo, it was difficult to understand exactly what was being said but I gathered they had been out on the town the previous night and were discussing what had happened.

It is a small space, so even if I wanted to, I could not switch off from hearing their chat. They met a group of girls and one of the two lads got a phone number but had lost it and was keen to contact this girl again. "No problem," said his buddy as he listed off ways his friend could try to trace her through Facebook, LinkedIn and other online sources. During their night out, they got separated from their buddies but found them again through Snapchat.

Got me thinking, things were a bit different in my day… One friend of mine met a girl out on a Saturday night and arranged to meet her the following Saturday outside the General Post Office (GPO). The other popular meeting spots in Cork were Brown Thomas (Cash's) or Debenhams (Roches Stores).

The only problem was he had a few drinks the previous week and could not remember exactly what she looked like. When he got to the GPO, there were five girls all waiting for their date to arrive. He walked around the block a few times trying to spot his woman. He eventually found her and today they are happily married with three children.

Even though things were different in our day, some things are just the same. Dating and business are very alike.

- A guy should know exactly what he wants (his target market).
- He has to get his marketing right (look good and create a good impression).
- Impress the girl (good presentation).
- She might not be too keen (handling objections).
- He wants to get her on a date (repeat business).

- And if things progress further, he will want to make sure the relationship is exclusive (keep the competition at bay).
- Later, they get married (customer for life).
- From the female perspective, she will want to avoid unsolicited approaches from men (spam).
- If a man looks the part, she will want to make sure he can hold a conversation (benefits as well as features).
- She must make sure she is not giving too much away (discounting).
- But of course, the most important thing for men and women is to stand out and be a bit different (USP).
- If a guy looks and acts the same as ten others, he won't stand out and will go home alone (no sales).

In business, a strong USP can make a huge difference in landing your ideal clients. Know what you do better than your competition and what is of real value to your customers. Put that USP in all your marketing, build it onto your sales message and most importantly, your price.

In lots of ways, business is very like dating.
You need to stand out from your competition (USP).

Have You Ever Been Barred from A Pub?

We went out for a few drinks one Friday night; nothing quite like that Friday feeling. We had a choice of sixty-odd pubs in the city centre. There were lots of trendy bars with modern décor and young friendly staff. But there was only one choice for us.

Up the stairs we went and opened the door into another world. The décor in this bar has not changed for eighty years. The music is classical. The gent's toilet is like a dungeon. The owner is an elderly man who is known far and wide. Some people call him eccentric. Others call him cantankerous. He runs the pub his way and is choosy about who he serves.

People have been barred from the pub for:
- Drinking too fast
- Drinking too slow
- Being too tall
- Drinking coke
- Complaining in any way, shape or form
- Using a mobile phone (another reason I like the place)

And of course, you may not have the opportunity to be barred if he does not like how you look and refuses to serve you. Almost everybody in the city has been either barred themselves or knows somebody who has. It is almost a badge of honour.

The bar is always busy. Why did we choose it? Because it has character. It is a small cosy pub and you will always get chatting to lots of people. Everybody has stories about the place and it is almost a competition to see who has the most outrageous one. Some drama is always just around the corner there.

There is a lesson here for us in business. We need to be different from our competition, stand out in some way, give people have a reason to choose you.

We could have chosen any one of sixty-odd pubs but to me, they all seemed similar. None of them stood out. If you think barring customers sounds strange, you probably need to lose some wasters like everybody else in business.

> **Give people a good reason to choose you over the competition.**

That Effin' Facebook

One morning I turned on the radio to hear them talking about 'Effin Facebook.' Now believe it or not, there is a place in Limerick called Effin. The local people were entering Effin in the 'Tidy Towns' competition and they wanted a Facebook page. But Facebook refused them. Obviously, they thought it was a bit close to a certain swear word. A local radio station heard the story and covered it. Then a local paper wanted it too.

Next there was a phone call from the BBC. Then some paper in New York. This story was covered all around the world. Facebook must have felt a bit embarrassed and they let the page go up.

What has all this got to do with business you might ask? Well, it is Public Relations (PR), isn't it? Free advertising.

And here is an interesting statistic:

A person reading a paper is four times more likely to believe a story or PR piece than they would an ad.

So how can you get some PR for your business? It is a lot easier than you might think. The papers and radio love a good news story especially if there is an unusual angle.

Let the papers and radio know if you have...

- Taken on a new member of staff.
- Launched a new product or service.
- Won a new account either in Ireland or outside it.
- Another tip is to put it into a format that the paper can just take and use. There are templates available online for this.

I hope to see you in the local paper soon.

If you have a good story which the media will run, it is like getting free advertising. This is PR.

How Quickly Can You Unfasten A Bra?

Sean Murray from Skibbereen is some man. He has just landed himself in the Guinness Book of Records for unfastening 91 bras in 60 seconds.

I wrote about this in a blog saying PR was like free advertising. I am sure his shop has been very busy over the last month since he announced his attempt.

There is another business lesson here too.

Sean could not find enough women volunteers for his record bid. But after being stuck for a while, he found a solution. He plugged the gap with men.

There was nothing in the rules saying the bra wearers had to be women. If you need to grow sales, maybe you need to broaden your target market, like the woman I worked with previously.

She was selling gluten-free bread at Farmer's Markets and while sales were good, she wanted to do better. She introduced a new delivery service and now supplies her breads to people who are too busy to go to Farmer's Markets.

Like Sean and his bra-wearing men, do you need to broaden your scope and find new target markets?

Good PR and a good title are not hard to find. You just need to keep your eyes open.

How to Get on National Radio

They say that PR is free advertising. Well, if that is the case I had loads of it one Friday. I was on the George Hook national radio show on Friday. He interviewed me about my new book, '*Why Social Media Does Not Work*.'

It is an interesting story, how it all came about. I was at a client meeting one Friday morning and I was telling the group about my plans to get media coverage for my book. We had a visitor there who mentioned that his niece was married to George Hook's son. As you may know, George Hook presents a chat show on Newstalk Radio every weekday.

After the network meeting, I rang the visitor who gave me the name of the chat show producer. I rang him about eleven and he asked me to email the book to him. They rang me back around three asking me if I would like to go on the show that evening and I said, 'Yes!'

This all happened very quickly and as I had not spoken on national radio before, I was slightly nervous. They said I would be on about 5.45pm and that the sound engineer would check with me beforehand.

I was expecting a call before this time and was waiting anxiously. My phone eventually rang about 5.44pm and I was told that the show had gone to ads and I was on in thirty seconds. A few more deep breaths to still the nerves and I was on. It seemed to go fine and as I was chatting to George on national radio, I actually felt quite calm.

After the call, I was inundated with texts, phone calls and emails saying things like 'well done,' 'you sounded very professional.'

As a business owner, what is the lesson here for you?

You probably know the old saying, 'there's a book in everybody.' When it comes to eBooks, I reckon there are lots of book in all of us. If you have a service business, you're selling knowledge so you certainly have lots of knowledge. And even if you sell products, rest assured you have lots knowledge to go with those items.

How do you produce an eBook?

If you have blogs, articles or any other content, that can be a good source. If you spoke for an hour, this can be transcribed into a twenty-page eBook.

Benefits of writing an eBook:

1. Additional sales.
2. Higher profile (somebody who writes a book is seen as an expert).
3. Increased traffic to your website.
4. Good PR is not that difficult to get.

Why Social Media Does Not Work

Social Media does not work for the vast majority of businesses. How do I know? Because I have worked with hundreds of them. I know lots of other people who work with similar businesses who would say the same thing.

When I say social media does not work, what I really mean is like all marketing, it needs to produce a return of additional sales and this is not happening for most businesses.

Before we go any further, let me clarify one thing. Social Media can work and I know of many businesses that have used it successfully to grow their sales.

So why does social media work for some business but not others? From my experience, there are three main reasons for this:

1. Time
2. Money
3. Expertise

Those businesses that use social media successfully have some combination of these three elements of time, money and expertise. Unfortunately, most small businesses are lacking in some or maybe all three elements. When I am talking about social media, I am referring to Facebook, Twitter, LinkedIn and Blogging.

3 Reasons Why Social Media Does Not Work

1. Time.

The majority of small businesses are one-man or one-woman bands. These people have limited time to invest in marketing their business. I would estimate that most business owners only invest between one and two hours per week marketing their business. This time is precious. For most people, social media is a steep learning curve. They must decide which one to use and then what is the best way of using it.

As many of these business people work alone, they must try to figure out themselves which is the best route for them. Unfortunately, many people seem to get stuck in selecting which media to use or in approaching the chosen one correctly. They put time and effort into this and get little or no return. Or they put time into it, see no return and stop.

2. Money.

In theory, people can invest time in social media and learn it themselves; in reality, this is easier said than done. As in many other areas in business and in life, sometimes the only realistic practical way to get a job done is to hire outside expertise. This is what many business people should do and would like to do but they cannot afford it. The reality of business for many business owners is that cash flow is tight and they do not have much money for investing in outside help and this includes social media.

3.   Expertise.

As mentioned above, social media is a new area of marketing and there is a lot to learn. The same way that many owners would not be able to design a website, equally they do not have the expertise to use social media to market their business.

It is a steep learning curve and as most have only two hours per week to spend on marketing and no budget to buy in expertise, they must try to learn it themselves. Some do so, but many unfortunately do not. The businesses that I see using social media effectively have some combination of expertise, time and money to invest in this area. Most small businesses lack some or all of these elements and hence get little or no return from social media.

Does social media work for you?
My experience is that it only works for one
business in every ten.
If it is not working for you, stop doing it and
try something else.

How Tweaking A Few Words Changes Everything

Please take a moment and look at the message below.

Message 1:

'Starting in 2 weeks, a course on **How to grow your sales.** *Runs for half a day per week for 5 weeks. Highly subsidised – just €125. Contact me if you would like more details. Neil.'*

I was due to run a course for a government agency and we only had a small number of people booked to attend. Seeing as it is a course on marketing, I said to myself, "I had better show them that I know what I am talking about, market this course and get some more bums on seats." I sent the first text message to about forty business people I know and waited for the response. And waited and waited... two hours later nobody had responded. I checked the phone to see if the message had gone alright and it had.

I looked at the message to see if some typo had changed the whole content – no. I looked at the message to see how I would feel if I received it. I actually thought it was a good message. As I had another forty business people to text, I decided that something would need to change. After thinking about it for a while, I came up with the second message below.

Message 2:

'Starting in 2 weeks, a course on **Zero Cost Marketing tips.** *Runs for half a day per week for 5 weeks. Highly subsidised – just €125. Contact me if you would like more details. Neil.'*

The eagle-eyed among you will note that the only change I made was to take out the title of 'How to grow your sales' and replace it with 'Zero Cost Marketing tips.'I sent the second message out to my other group of forty business owners and waited.

Within fifteen minutes, five people had texted back expressing an interest. Within another hour two more people texted. Most of those people signed up for the course. There are some important marketing lessons here.

1. If you are not sure whether to do A or B, why not do a split test, like the one above, do both and **let the market tell you** which one they prefer.

2. I spoke to two people last week who were unsure whether to use an ad and a flyer. They had thought about it for weeks and then did nothing. The most important thing about marketing is to **take some action**.

3. Marketing involves you investing either time or money. You must test the results and see what works best – **test and measure**. If I was marketing this course again, I would use the second message.

After the first text, I could have concluded that text messaging does not work for this course. But getting a zero-response rate is a result in itself and when I tweaked the next message, I got a great response. Marketing is a numbers game. While we can take an educated guess about what might work for us in marketing, there is only one way to find out for sure and that is by testing stuff and measuring the response.

Like the example above, my first text got zero-response (even though I thought it was a good message). I changed a few words, sent a second text and got a much better response. Our opinions can only tell us only so much about marketing. The only way to find out is to test the market.

> **To summarise, if you are not sure what to do in marketing, do something. Always test and measure, so you will know what works. If something works, do it again and again until it stops working.**

Cold Calling, A Forgotten Marketing Secret

With the advent of email and social media, some older marketing ideas are almost forgotten. Direct mail or to phone, then mail and phone again are very effective ways of getting sales. It may be hard work and not the most efficient use of time but it is tried and tested. When I started in business, obviously enough I had no customers to ask for referrals. And I had no referral sources to pass me warm leads. I used cold phone calls to successfully launch my business. This is how it worked...

I would get a list of businesses from the Golden Pages or some other source. I would phone the business to get the name of the owner or main decision-maker. I would send a letter and follow up a few days later with a phone call to see if I could book a sales meeting. I sent twenty letters every day and a few days later followed up with a phone call. The phone calls were 'fun' as the business owner did not know me and business coaching was quite new.

My Numbers Were Something Like This.

Weekly numbers
Letters sent: 100
Phone calls: 200
Sales meetings: 5
Clients signed: 1

So, on average, every 100 letters would get me five sales meetings and as sales was new to me then, I would sign up one new client from these meetings.

Now some people would look at these numbers and think they look really bad signing only one client from 100 letters. But I was thrilled with them. Why? Well, I knew that if I sent another 100 letters the following week, that I should sign another client. I did this for three months solid and signed twelve clients. Looking back on it now, I do not know how I did it. Having 95 out of 100 people tell you 'no' was not easy.

There are a couple of very important marketing lessons here.

Marketing, just like business, is a numbers game and you need to know your numbers. I knew mine and they were working, so I kept going. When you find something that works, keep doing it. I am a big fan of referrals, networking and warm leads but direct mail can still have its place. In fact, I will be doing some soon for the first time in years.

How many of your prospects get a hand-written envelope with a stamp? How many get a follow up phone call? Chances are your competition won't be doing this Once you know your target market, direct mail is very focused.

I was talking to a guy today who did it and from forty letters, he got one new client worth €10,000 per year (his ratio was better than mine, I had better have a chat with him). If relevant to your business, it might be worth considering.

> **Marketing, like all other aspects of business, is a numbers game and you need to know yours.**
> **When you have a specific target, a cold approach can work very well. That can be an e-mail, letter, phone call or some combination of all three.**

How to Score at the Disco

When I was a teenager (a few moons ago), going to the local disco was obligatory. What's not to like about teenage kids all self-conscious and spotty trying to pluck up the courage to ask a girl to dance during the 'slow set'?

One particular guy had a different approach to most. Let us call him Paul. When the slow set came on, boys and girls would separate, with the girls sitting down in one long row. At the start, there would only be a few couples on the dance floor, everybody could see everyone else. That is when Paul would make his move. He would start with the first girl in the row and ask her out. We could not hear what he was saying but we could all guess. He would move onto the second girl and then the third one.

It is safe to assume the conversation was something like this: "Would you like to dance?" asked Paul. "No," replied the girl.

And Paul kept going. By now he was on girl number ten and was still working his way down the line. And of course, everybody in the place was watching this with a mixture of amusement and disbelief. We were horrified that anybody would be so desperate to ask all these girls to dance. 'Has he no shame?' we would think. And then something strange would happen as Paul was no longer asking these girls to dance and was walking towards the dance floor with one of them. Girl number fifteen had said yes! Now we were all baffled beyond belief. Bad enough that he would ask all these women to dance but she was worse to say yes. Now remember this girl had seen Paul ask fourteen other girls to dance before asking her. But Paul got his dance and his girl. At the end of the night, when all the 'cool' guys were leaving on their own, Paul was leaving with girl number fifteen. And this was not an isolated case as Paul repeated his act every time we went to a disco.

What's this got to do with me and my business, you may well be asking? **When it comes to marketing, there are parallels between Paul's approach to asking girls to dance and direct marketing.**

As online marketing is very popular now, direct marketing like sending letters and email can seem old hat, but they can be very effective. The starting point for this is knowing your target market. Who is your main target market? Who are your most profitable customers? If you want to find more of them, then a direct approach can work well (just like Paul).

At the time of writing this book, I am getting my best results with businesses who have their own products and deliver great value to large pharmaceutical companies. I did this by driving around near one of my client's business with a Dictaphone and I recorded the names of those that looked like a good client for me. I ended up with fifty businesses and got online to find out what they do and the names of the main decision-makers. I always like referrals and am getting a warm introduction to about five of them. But that still leaves forty-five. I know where they are so I will start a campaign by sending emails to the decision-makers. Like Paul, I will get lots of no's but will also get a few yes's. How applicable is this to your business? If you know your best customers and want more, why not target them in some direct way like this? It worked for Paul at the disco and can work for you too. Note: When you were a teen and somebody's friend came over saying 'my friend likes you,' that is like a referral.

Like asking girls to dance, marketing is a bit of trial and error.
Like the example above, it is also a numbers game and you need to know yours to get the best return on your marketing spend and time.

Role Play Can Be Fun

Did a bit of role play earlier – no, not that kind of role play, it was in a training workshop.

One woman, Susan, wanted to target larger businesses on the phone. But we could sense she was a bit nervous about it. We did a bit of role play.

I got Susan to be the receptionist and asked another woman to be Susan. They were doing a role play of Susan phoning the business cold.

"Good morning, ABC Ltd," said the receptionist.

"Good morning, how are you keeping?" said Woman#1

"Very well, thank you – and you?" replied the receptionist.

"I'm keeping very well – thank you. What's your own name?" said Woman#1.

"Barbara," said the receptionist.

"Barbara, I wonder if you can help me. I'm just trying to find out if your company uses product X." asked Woman#1.

"I think we do but I would have to double check," said Barbara, the receptionist.

"Ok Barbara, if you could that would be great. I'm just looking to send some information into the business," said Woman#1.

And it continued like this for a while.

The role play was very informative for Susan. By playing the receptionist role she could step into the shoes of the other person. The woman playing Susan took a very softly-softly approach. She was not trying to sell anything, just find out if the company used product X. And if they did, she would send some information to the decision-maker.

> **Doing research before launching any sales initiative is a good approach. Find out what the companies needs first. And find out the name of the decision-maker. What is most people's favourite word? Their own name. Use it.**

The woman playing Susan above had lots of experience of making calls like this. She used Barbara's name quite a lot. This is very important in most conversations of this type.

Although cold calling seems like it is a thing of the past, it can still play a vital role in some marketing plans.

Cold calling can be very targeted, and like all other marketing it is a number game. For every X numbers of calls you will get a sales meeting/quotation or whatever. From every X number of sales meetings you will get a sale.

Fill in the X's above for your business and you know your key marketing numbers. And this applies to any other marketing initiatives. Happy phoning.

> **The best way to learn cold calling is to get on the phone and practice. Have a bit of fun with it. It is a great skill to have and is not as daunting as most people believe.**

Marketing Lessons From R.E.M.

Years ago, I received an email from X Promotions. X are big concert promoters. I was really surprised as I had never got an email from X before. I did not even know they had my email. They were promoting an R.E.M. concert. The tickets were going on sale in two days' time. They were giving me an opportunity to buy tickets before they went on sale to the public. I have been a big fan of R.E.M. for years. Most people remember 'Losing my religion' as their first big hit, but that single was on their seventh studio album. R.E.M. had been around for ten years before that and I have been a fan since day one. Anyway, I was trying to think where X got my email address. And then I realised that I had booked tickets for R.E.M. online a couple of years earlier. Obviously, I must have booked the tickets for R.E.M. through X. Two years later, X are promoting an R.E.M. concert. Think about R.E.M. for a moment and how this applies to your business. This is worth repeating – these concert promoters are not stupid.

Who is most likely to buy your product again? Somebody who bought your product previously.

Of course, I probably would not have bought those R.E.M. tickets if I had not received that email. And your customers may not buy if they do not get an email, text, letter or whatever is the most suitable way for you to remind them to come back and buy from you again. Some of your customers may come back and buy from you already. And that is great. I think of it as organic or natural. But do you have a system for reminding your customers that you exist? Do you have a system to tell them when you have a sale, promotion or special offer? If you do, more of them will come back and buy from you again. These are **new extra sales** on top of the organic, natural ones you get already. Remember R.E.M., make the effort and sales will automatically follow, just like night follows day.

A good database of customers is like a goldmine, if it is used.
Like me getting an email and going to the R.E.M. concert, your customers may not buy from you again, without some encouragement to do so.

Opera Lovers

I got a letter in the post. I opened it up to be greeted by 'Dear Opera Lover.' Must be the wrong address, I thought to myself. No, I checked the envelope and there was my name and address on the front. Then I had a flashback to getting something similar in the post in recent weeks.

Now, let me share with you my brief history with opera. My sister loves it and dragged me along to some performance years ago. Luckily there were some other friends of hers with us. I say luckily because half way through the performance I fell asleep – literally. That will tell you my interest in opera. That was my one and only show. And that was over ten years ago. And it was booked through my sister so they do not have my details.

This is marketing. Not very effective marketing, if you ask me. I am not an opera lover, as they seem to believe. I will never darken their door. Yet they are wasting time and money sending out this info to me. Now my sister lives close by, is an opera lover, and she got no letter. They were missing from school the day this marketing lesson was covered.

'Get your marketing message in front of your target market.'

This business has a database but it seems hopelessly inaccurate. My email titled 'No Mushrooms Allowed' got a big reaction. Maybe the opera people should learn a bit more about mushrooms. You must know your target market and get your message in front of them. I am getting their opera letter when I will never buy from them, while my sister, the opera lover, gets no letter from them. This should not be difficult to get right.

Note: Keep details of what your customers buy, and send them regular offers with similar products. Amazon do this brilliantly.

Years ago, I bought tickets from R.E.M. online. Two years later, I got an email from X Promotions. Guess who was coming to town? R.E.M. Guess who bought a ticket to see them again?

Do you have a database of your customers?

Do you have details of previous purchases they made?

Do you keep in regular contact with these people, giving them the opportunity to buy again?

Please remember the opera people – and do the opposite. The R.E.M. and mushroom people have it sussed.

How Amazon Crushes Waterstones

Recently I got an email from Waterstones with details of their latest bestsellers. I have particular authors I like and they are generally not bestsellers. The previous week, the Opera House sent me details of a Shakespeare poem thingy. Not my scene. Both of these approaches are a bit like trying to sell meat to a vegetarian.

When Bob Rotella brings out a new golf book, Amazon email me. I am into golf and may buy his new book. This is akin to selling meat to a meat eater.

I am a regular customer of Waterstones, the Opera House and Amazon. They all know my tastes (or should do). If Waterstones were on the ball, they should know I like Cormac McCarthy novels and personal development books. But they have never emailed me about these, likewise with the Opera House.

But Amazon are different. They take the time and trouble to make a note of my purchases and send me emails with similar material.

Amazon have built a massive business with this approach. It is not that difficult to keep track of your customer's purchases and communicate with them about similar products. Email is the easiest, cheapest and most effective way of doing it.

Do you have a database of your customers? If you are in contact with them, are you more like Amazon or Waterstones?

What is stopping you from doing what Amazon does so well?

Keep track of your customer's preferences and offer them similar products. And watch the boost in your sales.

> **Amazon take the time and trouble to note what you have bought before and can recommend similar purchases. If you can do this with your customers, it will lead to extra sales. Are you willing to invest that time?**

Margaret Thatcher Upset the Hairy French Bikers

Margaret Thatcher is still upsetting people, even years after her death. And I am not even talking about her advice to Peter Mandelson when he became the Northern Ireland Minister. He revealed that her only advice to him was: 'Don't trust the Irish – they're all liars.'

She has upset some big hairy French bikers. This is what happened: Lorraine, who is part of an online forum I am joined, shared a story with us. She sent an email to her list. In the email, she spoke about Margaret Thatcher and some of her positive qualities. Qualities like determination and loyalty.

Her email list is made up of French vintage motorcycle customers. She did not say this but I have an image of hairy leather clad French men. And she is telling them how marvellous she thinks Margaret Thatcher really was.

I think you might see where this is going...

She got six stinking emails from French socialist bikers:

'What are you thinking?' 'Do you not realise how Thatcher had ruined the working classes?'

This may seem very negative, but Lorraine's list had 2,500 people. Six out of 2,500 really is a tiny percentage. Lorraine was worried she had upset these people. She was reassured by people in the group that she had nothing to be worried about. She would get some unsubscribes. But this is not a negative thing – this is positive. An email list needs new people in and some old ones out.

This view is the total opposite to the one most business people express. This is the gist of a conversation I have had many times before:

"How many email addresses do you have?" I ask.

"About 1,000," replies the client.

"Great. How often do you email them?" I probe.

"Twice a year," says the client.

"What response do you get?" I ask.

"Sales go up by about 30% that week," reveals the client.

"That's' great. Why don't you email them more often?" I ask.

"I can't, it will only annoy them," says the client.

If somebody gives you their email address, they expect to get emails from you. I am not saying email them daily but 'the more often the better' is my motto. If people do not want your message, they will unsubscribe. These people were unlikely to buy from you again anyway.

Do you have a list of email or mobile numbers you are not using? Or not using very often? To me that is a bit like buying a new car but not driving it as you do not want to wear out the tyres.

More emails and texts to your customers mean more sales for you. It isn't rocket science.

Do not be afraid of unsubscribes

Many business owners are afraid of unsubscribes, hence they do not use their database. As somebody once said, 'It is a bit like not breathing to conserve oxygen. It works for a short while and then you die.'

If you have an email list, not all of these people will buy from you again. But some of them will buy and indeed a small percentage may buy everything you ever have. But you will never know who they are if you do not email them. The price of this is unsubscribes. But you can't get one without the other, like you can't make an omelette without cracking some eggs. The same logic applies to texting, writing letters, etc.

> **A database is meant to be used – regularly,
> just like a car is meant to be driven.
> Get driving that database.**

Ice Bucket Challenge Business Lessons

Unless you've been living under a rock or returned from outer space, you will have seen the mad craze that swept the world a few years back. It is called the 'Ice bucket challenge,' where a friend challenges you to pour a bucket of iced water over your head.

You must record the event, post it on Facebook and nominate three people you know to do the same thing and they in turn will name three of their friends and so on. Everybody who does the challenge must donate €2 to Motor Neuron Disease, which is a very good cause.

It is amazing how some things take off and others do not.

I think one of the reasons this has taken off is because everybody knows three people they can nominate – it is tapping into people's network. Funny how tapping into somebody's network can work very well. And there is a great business lesson here.

Guess who else knows at least three people and has a big network? Your customers.

Satisfied customers can become a sales team for your business.

Hopefully you get referrals already and business from word of mouth. This is great. But I am talking about something else. I am talking about adding onto your current level of sales. This sales team won't happen by itself. You need to play your part by encouraging this team.

Just giving out your business card or brochure to customers and saying, 'Please pass on to anybody you know,' is just too hopeful an approach to marketing. Your cards may soon be filed in the bin. On a regular basis, you need to ask your customers for referrals. You need to get names of people they know and tap into their network. And you need to get your customers to contact these people and start the selling process.

I meet a lot of resistance when I discuss this with clients. They think this is pushy. They do not feel comfortable doing this.

So, let me ask you one question.

If your customers are happy with your service, why would they not want to tell their suppliers and other business contacts about you?

If you helped them save money or with some other issue, do your customers know other people that you could also help?

Referrals from customers is the most successful marketing strategy I have ever used. In an eighteen-month period, it brought me in over €60,000 worth of sales. My clients became my sales team.

Like the ice bucket challenge tapped into people's network to pick three people, you too can tap into your customer's network to grow your sales. Invest time talking to your customers and they can bring new customers to you.

There is A Man in My Gutters

Last Saturday morning I was pottering around my house, when I heard a knock at my front door. I opened the door to see a guy in white t-shirt and jeans with flyers in his hands looking up at my gutters. Ok, he wasn't quite in my gutters but he looked like he wanted to have a nose around them all the same.

Ok, no prizes being given out for guessing what he was selling. He mumbled something about gutters and power washing. I muttered something back at him about my brother doing it, which he does and off the man went.

Maybe you do not encounter this situation too often but I do almost every week. How do you react when some stranger knocks on your door like this selling stuff? I call tell you what went through my head: 'I do not know who you are. I do not know what kind of job you would do. Who else have you done this for? What would you charge me?'

What lessons are there here for us business owners?

Like me (the customer) standing there looking at this guy (the seller), are there situations when your potential customer is looking at you with similar questions in their head?

Who is this person? Who else has he/she worked with? Will he/she do a good job? What will he/she charge?

The solution for you is similar to the one that I would suggest to gutter-man. If gutter-man had knocked on my door and said something like: 'Hi, Neil, is it? Hi, my name is John Murphy and here's my business card. If you're wondering how I got your name, John from number six gave it to me. I asked him if he knew anybody else who might be interested in getting some cleaning done. I did some work for John at number six and Mary at number twenty-seven and they were both very happy. They mentioned your name as being somebody who might be interested. I will be here again all day next Saturday and maybe during the week if you see John or Mary they could tell you what I did for them.'

Now if gutter-man had taken this approach, he would have gotten a warmer reception from me. Also, if I was interested in getting some jobs done – and who doesn't have jobs that need to be done around the house? I would have a week to talk to John or Mary. And gutter-man was back next week and would probably call on my door. Or I could phone and book him in.

We can all learn lessons from gutter-man on how not to do it.

Use a warm introduction to get more sales.

Why Abba Are the Poor Man's Beatles

It seems everywhere you looked in the noughties, Abba appeared. First the musical, then the movie, followed by the museum.

Now do not get me wrong, Abba was a good group. 'Dancing Queen' is probably their best song. Good as the song is, it might just scrape into a Beatles Top 20. You see, while Abba were a good group, they were only trotting after The Beatles – not fit to lace their boots.

Take the best parts of 'Dancing Queen', multiply it by one hundred and you have The Beatles. Without The Beatles, there would be no Abba, or Oasis or…

It is difficult to even attempt to describe their music. All I know it is that is it is uplifting, energetic and passionate. It is puts a smile on my face, gets my energy levels up and puts me in a good mood, without fail – every single time.

Yet anybody born after 1990 may be under the false impression that Abba are better than The Beatles. Sacrilege.

Why? Because of the attention and hype that is surrounds them. What's the lesson here? You do not have to be the best to be considered the best. I regularly hear idiots on the radio who do not know their arse from their elbow yet they are considered experts in their field. How do they get on the radio? You see there are 'expert' roles in most fields. And they somehow managed to get that slot.

In your business, there are slots for so-called experts. Are they all gone or could you grab one? I am not suggesting that you go waffling on the local radio, you need to know your stuff. If you've been in business for any length of time, you have expert knowledge in your area.

How do get that expert role?
➢ Write articles.
➢ Get on the radio.
➢ Get in your local paper.
➢ Get speaking engagements.
➢ Write a book or an eBook.

Any combination of these can get you seen as an expert. This can have big benefits for your business. I wrote an eBook last year and got on national radio.

> **Believe me, if people think Abba are better than The Beatles, anything is possible. You do not have to be the best to be seen as the best.**

Business Is Just Like Dating

It may not seem obvious to most people but business and dating are very alike, especially when it comes to the marketing side of business. Seth Godin is one of the most influential business authors of the past few decades. His ground-breaking book '*Permission Marketing*' changed how many businesses approached marketing with some staggering results.

Have you ever been sitting down having your dinner, when the phone rings and some stranger is trying to sell you a phone service or cheaper electricity? Any time we watch television for ten or fifteen minutes, the programme will stop to show ads which run for three to five minutes. Your favourite soap has been interrupted by ads. In his book, Seth calls this 'interruption marketing.' He advocates a different approach where people give their permission to receive information. Have you ever given your email address to get a free product online? This is an example of permission marketing.

The idea with permission marketing is that you do not try to sell to a prospect straight away. Instead you give them useful information and over time educate them about the benefits of your product or service. Then at some later stage you try to make the first sale. And this is the start of a long fruitful relationship as if you keep providing useful information, then at regular intervals your customer should buy from you. And this is where the dating analogy comes in.

Permission marketing is a bit like dating. Two strangers meet and go on a first date. If it goes well, the two of them go on another date. And then another. Until after ten or twelve dates, both sides can really communicate with each other about their needs and desires.

Permission marketing turns strangers into friends and friends into lifetime customers. Many of the rules of dating apply, as do many of the benefits. The incentive you offer the customer can range from information to entertainment, to a sweepstake, to outright payment for the prospect's attention. But the incentive must be overt, obvious and clearly delivered.

One of the goals is to motivate a consumer to give more permission over time. Permission to gather more data about the customer's personal life or hobbies or interests. By doing this, a business can get very specific about the messages and products it offers its customers.

Five Steps To Dating Your Customer:

1. Offer a prospect an incentive to volunteer information.
2. Using the attention offered by the prospect, offer a curriculum over time, teaching the consumer about your product or service.
3. Reinforce the incentive to guarantee the prospect maintains the permission.

4. Offer additional incentives to get even more permission from the consumer.
5. Over time, leverage the permission to change consumer behaviour towards profits.

There are many ways to approach permission marketing but the one you are probably most familiar with is email marketing. If you're a regular reader of my emails, you will know I am a big fan as it works very well in many ways. It is successful in getting extra sales from new and existing customers, in educating people about the benefits of your services and in building strong relationships with loyal customers, some of whom will buy again and again.

> **Business is very like dating.**
> **You will get better results when you ask for permission.**
> **Do this with your marketing and you can build great**
> **relationships with customers who buy from you again and**
> **again.**

50% Of People Never Do This

50% of people will do this, and 50% of people will not. What am I talking about? 50% of people will never buy from you, regardless of what you do.

Now for the good news.

5% of people will buy from you all the time. They will buy your new products. They will buy special offers. They will buy in summer time, in winter time. I think you get the picture.

Those who are good at maths will realise there are 45% of people left. So, what about them? Somewhere between 0% to 45% may buy from you again.

What will this percentage be? Nobody can tell you that.

But I can tell you what will affect the number – how often you contact them, the quality of your message, having special offers (we all like them).

Let us say you have five hundred email addresses or mobile numbers, and you contact these people twice a year, then your percentage of extra people buying may not be huge.

But if you contact them every month, you will get extra sales. Remember people buy when they are ready – not when you want to sell them.

The more often you contact people, the greater the chance that some of them are ready to buy from you.

Let us summarise what this means for your business. Let us say you have lots of client email addresses you do not use, or a bunch of mobile numbers. If you start regular contact with them and have a product offer somewhere in there, 5% of those people will buy pretty soon. And if you keep regular contact, more will buy from you. How many more? I am not sure exactly but it is somewhere between 0% and 45%.

Now you may never get them all. Let us say you get 15%. That is on top of the 5% you are almost guaranteed. That is an extra 20% sales, just from using those email addresses you already have.

Take those business cards gathering dust and start doing something with them. And I wonder why people still say business is hard. Just do it. Or as they say on my forum – JFDI.

> **50% of your customers may buy from you again. The best, easiest and cheapest way to encourage them is through e-mail marketing.**

Amazing Numbers

The numbers below are from a marketing campaign run in recent years. I got these numbers when I attended a webinar last year hosted by Daniel Lewis.

The woman in question had an online 'Weight loss' product. She got sales of just over $30,000 from the campaign. As you can guess from the description below, it was an email campaign.

I appreciate the numbers may be difficult to follow so I will describe the main learnings I took from them.

1. She sent fifteen emails in an eight-day period and got sales of over $30,000.

2. You might think most of the sales would come at the start or end of the campaign but her biggest sales were $6,750 and they came from the eighth email she sent. Why did that email bring in such a high level of sales? No-one knows for sure.

3. You might think sending many emails would annoy people and that if they wanted the product, they would have bought it after the first email.

She got sales from thirteen of the fifteen emails. How can this be explained? Maybe people need to see a message a few times before they buy. Maybe people missed the earlier emails.

4. Were lots of people annoyed and did they unsubscribe after getting fifteen emails in eight days? 427 people unsubscribed over the eight days which is about 3.2% of her total email list of 13,500 at the start of the campaign.

5. Because she has an opt-in box on her website, over the same eight days, 409 new people joined her email list; her total number was almost the same at the end as the beginning.

6. When sending fifteen emails, people may think everybody who wanted to buy would do so early on but that is not taking the urgency factor into account. 'Sale ends in 2 days' is often used by shops to inject urgency. The same is true with email and they got over $4,900 in sales from the last three emails.

I am not sure what you think on reading this and looking at the numbers but I was amazed when I first saw them. It blows an awful lot of the email marketing myths out of the water.

Are you afraid to e-mail customers too often in case you annoy them?
These numbers clearly demonstrate that, once someone has given you permission, they do not mind getting lots of e-mails from you.

Make Money While Playing Golf

I made some nice money while playing golf one Friday. If you have seen my golf, you would know it was not through a bet on our match (Rory McIlroy is quite safe).

My promotion on my email marketing product was finishing at 5pm on that Friday and I was playing golf at 4pm.

Luckily with Mailchimp and all similar products, you can schedule emails to go whenever you like. Businesses can write a sequence of thirty emails in advance and once you're added to their email list, you will get one email per day for thirty days and for that last week, they may be promoting a product on special offer.

This is an example of a 'passive income' where the money comes in and you have no work to do, except check your bank balance every so often. That must be the ideal business to have. Imagine being on holidays, away for a weekend or out for a nice meal and it could all be paid for, without you lifting a finger.

I am not there yet but I got a glimpse of it on that Friday while I was playing golf. I was checking my email and sales were coming in. Now that was a nice feeling (especially as my golf was crap).

I promised to share some lessons from that week's promotions, so here goes…

Have you heard the saying, 'Most sales happened after the fifth no.'? Which means somebody can try to sell to you four times and you say no but the fifth time you say yes. Only 2% of sales happen first time round. The message in those figures is to follow up and keep asking for the sale. Most people stop after the first or second no.

I sent six emails in six days. On the last day, I sent four emails, each one stressing that time was running out. 'Only two hours left to avail if this bargain!' Now some people find this pushy but it is using urgency. On the Friday, I got 83% of the total sales and most of them came with the final email (80:20 at work again).

There is a big lesson here for me and you in every sales situation (and not just product sales). People respond to urgency. Those stats of following up are so true. I asked for the sale ten times and most people responded on the ninth and tenth time. Why? Because if they hesitated, the chance was gone. Most people do not buy first time.

Think about your own business for a moment.

How often do you follow up, if a person does not buy first time? Do you take people's contact details so you can follow up if they do not come back and buy from you? Do you keep details of people who do not buy and have a system in place to make sure you follow up?

The more marketing you do the better. Initially I was just e-mailing my list but the response was slow and I decided to add some more marketing.

- ➤ I created blogs and posted them to my website.
- ➤ I posted these blogs in LinkedIn, Facebook and Twitter.
- ➤ I set up some Facebook ads which brought quite a few people to my landing page.
- ➤ I anticipated sending all those emails that I would have some unsubscribes. I had three over the week with two new people joining, overall, I was down one person.

> ➢ I am now adding products to my service business and will be doing a lot more of it (you have been warned).

Whether you have a service or product business, you could do the same.

Do something once and sell it for years to come.

All my work is done on this and any sales in the future are 100% profit. And it is adding to my existing 'service' income.

Do you ever dream about retiring early to Spain? You will probably have to add products to your business model to do this. Imagine how good that would feel… Lying on the beach in Spain, knowing you were making sales and the cash was coming in. This is very doable. Enjoy the sunshine (and think of Spain).

How often do you follow up, if a person does not buy first time? **Do you take people's contact details so you can follow up if they do not come back and buy from you?** **Do this and your conversion rate and sales will increase –** **guaranteed.**

A Simple Way To Grow Sales

One thing amazes me about business. Most great ideas are really simple. Yet most people will not do them. Fear is a huge factor in business and in life in general.

I am going to share something with you. And I do so knowing this will work for your business. Yet most people won't do this. If more than one in ten does this, I will be shocked (please prove me wrong and email me when you do it).

Here are two case studies from my online forum:

1.   Training Company

Clive had a training company and he deals mostly with schools. He was putting his prices up next week and of course this will boost his profits for years to come. But before he put them up, he emailed his list and offered them a chance to buy at the old prices. He ran this promotion for a week and gave schools the chance to buy at the 'old prices.' These schools were a mixed bag. Some were past customers and others were current. Some were prospects and others have looked at his courses before and declined.

Before I tell you the answer, how do you think this promotion went? How might it go for your business?

Clive has set a stretch sales target of £500,000 and is just starting his year. During the last week, he got £250,000 worth of orders. That is half his target of the year. What an amazing result? Clever but in other ways very simple.

> **He is using psychology that is as old as mankind. It is called the 'takeaway.' Offer something for a limited time and then it is gone up to the higher price.**

2. Hairdresser

The second case study involves Monica who owns a hairdressing salon. She did the same thing and ran an email/text campaign telling her customers that prices were going up next week and this was the last chance to book at the old prices. She allowed people to book a few months ahead at the old prices.

She took €75,000 in bookings.

Could you do this? Why not do it with a selection of your products and see how it goes. Or better still, do it with all your products.

> **This tactic is genius. Not only does it have one of my favourite business tips, increase prices, but it also introduces urgency and takeaway selling. This idea may pack in more different strategies than any other that I know.**

SECTION 4 MINDSET

MINDSET MAKES THE DIFFERENCE

Kissing George Clooney

Listening to the radio one day I heard a report that George Clooney was spotted in Blarney the previous weekend. The report added that a local woman called Michelle had snatched a kiss from George. I know a Michelle from Blarney and she is an extrovert so it did not seem completely implausible.

When I saw Michelle in the supermarket, I asked her the question that any woman in the world would love to hear.

"Are the rumours about yourself and George Clooney true?" I asked. "Yes, they are," said Michelle laughing. She then proceeded to tell me what had happened.

She was working in a café in the village and heard a bit of commotion. She looked over and saw somebody who looked like George Clooney. She could see other people looking in his direction but none of them were approaching him. Michelle isn't shy. She walked over towards him and called his name. 'George,' she said.

He turned around smiling and she went over and said, 'Welcome to Ireland!' and placed a quick kiss on his cheek.

He smiled, laughed and said, 'Thank you very much!'

"Michelle," I said, "you're the envy of every woman in the world." The people who stood around and did nothing were probably thinking, 'Is it him or not? What would I say to him? How will he react?'

Michelle didn't over-analyse the situation but took action – she walked over and got the result – a kiss from one of the hottest men on the planet.

As I was walking back from the supermarket I was thinking that there are marketing lessons here for business owners. When it comes to marketing, many business owners are like the people who stood looking at George and had not taken action. Will I send a letter or email? When is the best time to send it? What will I say?

People over-analyse the situation and end up doing nothing. They need to be more like Michelle – take action and see what result they get.

Test and measure. If it works, do it again. If it does not work either tweak and try it again or do something else and measure the result.

> **Many people procrastinate over which action to take and end up doing nothing. They could learn from Michelle who did not think about the situation for too long and just took action.**

Irish People and the Weather

This is the great topic of conversation in Ireland and it cracks me up on a regular basis – people's mindset around the weather. It says a lot about their outlook on life.

Exhibit A: Yesterday in my local supermarket
"It's a scorching day out there," I said
"Tis but there's a shocking breeze. At least it's not raining

anyway," said the assistant. (It is one of the warmest days of the year but do not worry, I'll make sure I mention the rain anyway).

Exhibit B: On numerous occasions in April
"Hope you're enjoying the nice weather," I said.
"This is powerful but I'm afraid this is going to be our summer," said the assistant. (This is April and we haven't got near May, June, July or August but Mr Optimistic reckons our summer will end on the 30th April).

Exhibit C Last year in the middle of our finest summer for twenty years.
"The weather is great but we'd want it. Do you remember last summer? We nearly got washed away. It was unbelievable!" said my client. (We might be after three months of constant sunshine but do not worry, I will make sure I mention all that rain from last year.)

I hear these types of comments all the time. Now you might think people are just being polite and making conversation. I would view it differently.

They are born pessimists, glass half empty type of people. Their beliefs influence everything in their lives. What they do. Where they work. What they earn. Who they marry. And so on. What's that got to do with me?' you may well be asking. 'Everything,' is the answer.

Studies have found that only 1 in 100 business owners ever reach financial independence.

That means they could stop work tomorrow and never worry about money again. The other 99% vary from struggling to just doing ok. The 1% who are successful would not think like the people in the supermarket. Studies have found the 1% are not better educated or intelligent than the 99%. But they do think and act differently. Some are born that way but most work on improving how they think. They become more aware of any self-limiting beliefs and self-talk. Maybe their mindset in business was like those people in the shop but they became aware of it and changed their beliefs.

Have you ever had a good idea but then thought that you lacked the knowledge or experience to pursue it and did nothing?

Test Your Mindset Exercise

How much money did you earn last year?

What if I told you that you could earn your annual income every month?

What is your initial reaction to this statement? Do you accept it is possible and want to explore how you can do it? Or did you dismiss it out of hand and think, 'That's impossible for me!'?

If the latter is your reaction, then you are more than likely in the group of 99%. You do not have to be there forever but it will take quite a bit of work to make the transition.

Successful people visualize their success before it ever happens. And they have a strong belief that it will happen. This preview of their future life is what gets them through the tough times. It helps them make the right decisions.

> **We need to change on the inside before our outer world will change. Your attitude to the weather, the government and your neighbour's dog can be all be an indication of your mindset. To be successful in business, you must have the right mindset.**

Suarez Biting Incident

Without doubt, the main story in the 2014 World Cup was Luis Suarez biting his Italian opponent during their world cup match. Everybody seemed to have an opinion from 'Ban him for life' to 'He needs help.' Plenty of people called his biting act 'barbaric.' Even one of his Uruguayan team mates mentioned barbaric. I had to do a double take on that one because all his team mates supported him. Incredibly Lugano, the Uruguay captain, called the four-month ban of Suarez barbaric. It has been one of the more interesting aspects of the whole incident for me, how his Uruguayan team mates, management and even the president of the country supported him.

Is this blind loyalty or do they really believe Suarez did not bite his opponent? While the rest of the world condemned Suarez for his act, Uruguay and its people stood squarely behind him. Their belief seemed hard to comprehend yet appeared very strong.

Our beliefs are powerful things. Many of them are picked up when we are young from teachers, parents, priests and other people of authority. Many of these beliefs stay with us for life.

113

Just think about religious or political beliefs. Despite all the controversies over religion and politicians, many people do not waver in their beliefs.

We always act in a way consistent with our beliefs.

If somebody who believes they are big boned and can't lose weight, goes on a diet, guess what? That person will not lose weight. I was a smoker for years and tried giving up a few times. Once I was off them for eighteen months but during that time, I still wanted to smoke and eventually went back on them. Then about fifteen years ago, I read a book called '*The Easy Way to Stop Smoking*' by Allan Carr. This book did not use willpower but tackled the beliefs most smokers have, such as: 'John up the road lived until he was ninety and he had smoked every day.' 'I won't enjoy my holidays if I'm not smoking,' and lots more. One in two smokers die young, John up the road is an exception. Plenty of people enjoy their holidays, without smoking.

This book took all my beliefs around smoking and challenged them. Shortly after reading the book, I quit smoking. And it felt different from previous attempts, which had used willpower alone. On those previous attempts, when I saw my friends smoking in the pub, I still wanted one. After reading Allan Carr's book and changing my beliefs, my attitude to smoking changed. When I saw my friends smoke while having a drink, I felt sorry that they were addicted to that disgusting habit. Changing my beliefs around smoking changed my actions. Previous attempts had worked on willpower alone. Willpower alone will not bring any lasting change.

If you want to change any result in your life, you first need to change your beliefs.

Only 1% of business owners ever hit the nirvana of financial independence, which means they could stop working and never have to worry about money again. These people are not more intelligent or have any other special qualities compared to the other 99%. But they do think differently. Their belief systems are different. And the good news is anybody can change their beliefs. But like giving up smoking or losing weight, it can take some work. But it is doable. In business when an opportunity comes along, do you find yourself saying, 'I do not have the experience!' or 'I could never do that?' Awareness is key to changing beliefs. You need to become aware of the conversations you have in your head at these times and change them.

> To change any result in your life, you must first change your beliefs. If you want to grow your sales or take a bigger wage from your business, first you need to tackle these beliefs that are holding you back.

What Little Johnnie Did in School

Johnnie was a six-year-old boy who really liked school but he struggled with maths. His teacher told him he was no good at maths. His parents told him he would never be good at maths. His fellow pupils told him...

I think you get the picture.

For most of his time in school, he did not like maths and struggled with them. This was fuelled by his belief that he was 'no good at maths.' This was his 'story' about maths.

Then one day, the teacher put a tough maths puzzle up on the board and asked the class if anybody could solve it. After looking at it for a few moments, and to his own amazement, Johnnie realised he could solve the tough problem.

Johnnie put up his hand saying, "I can solve it!" but the teacher just laughed at him. He persisted and put up his hand again and this time all his classmates laughed.

At this stage, he was growing more frustrated and annoyed. He marched to the top of the class, grabbed the chalk and to everybody's amazement, he solved the problem.

Johnnie was not bad at maths. In fact, he was very good at maths. But because he was a slow learner when younger, he was told by teachers, parents and students that he was no good at maths. All of this formed his belief that he was no good at maths and we always act in a way consistent with our beliefs. Johnnie continued to be poor at maths because that is what he told himself, that is what he believed. And he could have gone through life thinking that way if it was not for that day in class.

This story is from a great book written by Maxwell Maltz called, '*Psycho-Cybernetics.*' This book talks a lot about our beliefs and self-image. Beliefs are powerful. They are often formed when we are young. And we do not choose them – just like Johnnie, our beliefs are often formed by teachers, parents and other figures of authority and influence. That day in class changed Johnnie's life. He went on to have a very successful career as a maths professor.

What has all this got to do with me, you may well be asking. And the answer is *everything*. Your beliefs shape everything about your life. Your business, relationships, religious beliefs, politics, etc.

Why are some people successful while many others struggle to take their business onto another level?

Your beliefs can hold you back, like an anchor.

I have studied this topic extensively over the past year and made a major breakthrough in recent weeks. Awareness of our beliefs is a lifelong journey and I still have a long way to go.

So, what was my breakthrough?

When I was challenged by something, I simply wrote down my negative beliefs and challenged them. If I was saying to myself, 'you do not have the experience to do X,' I listed off the different times I had done X, which meant I had plenty of experience.

Quite often our beliefs have no basis in facts and won't stand up to much scrutiny.

You might remember this the next time you have a challenge – maybe a new customer or a new service you're thinking of doing. It could be a marketing piece.

I have sent emails telling how vouchers or asking for referrals can really boost sales. What did you say to yourself when you read that? Is it 'My business is different, that would never work!' or maybe 'My customers wouldn't like that!' or 'I couldn't do that!'

Like me, you are not short of ideas to grow your sales. The biggest obstacle to your business may well be what you see in the mirror every morning. If you can understand these beliefs and control them, you can have the business and lifestyle of your dreams.

Please keep this email in mind and challenge your beliefs the next time they try to stop you.

Our beliefs are powerful and like an anchor, they can hold us back in life. Like Johnnie when he marched to the board, if we challenge our beliefs, we can transform our lives.

A Young Girl Playing Piano

At a school concert recital, a young girl was playing piano. She had been playing piano for several years and had practiced very hard for the concert. She was to play four songs.

She played the first two songs confidently and the audience, which of course included her proud parents, were really enjoying it. After the second song, she looked out at the audience and smiled. As she did so, she noticed a man in the front row yawning. The young girl frowned. Then she started thinking. "Why is that man yawning? He must be bored. He is bored with my playing. I'm not a very good piano player."

The girl played her final two songs but her concentration was broken and she made several mistakes. When finished, she rushed off the stage crying.

The young girl saw something, a man yawning, and made a whole set of assumptions from that, without any evidence to back it up. The man could have been tired or the room might have been too warm.

Why am I sharing this story with you?

It is an example of how our minds can work. You may be thinking 'not me, my mind doesn't work that way' but we all make somewhat similar assumptions.

> **In business, understanding how we think is what distinguishes the successful from the rest.**

Think about your own business for a moment. When a new idea or opportunity comes along, how do you think?

Do you ever find yourself saying…
- 'I do not have the experience.
- 'That would never work in my business.'
- 'I'd look foolish if that didn't work.'

I know I have in the past.

Like the young girl above playing piano, we can all make assumptions based on no real evidence. This is our fears kicking in trying to protect us.

Everybody has fears but it is how we respond to them, is what is most important. Tiger Woods once said, that the day he does not feel any fear on the first tee, is the day he quits golf.

The most successful business people have the same fears as you and me. Richard Branson, Michael O'Leary and Bill Gates all have fears. But they also have ways of recognising these fears. They do not allow these fears to stop them doing the right things in business.

I see fears all the time with clients, especially when it comes to putting up prices and asking customers for referrals. When I say to a client 'put up your prices 10%,' they think 'I will lose all my customers.' But they are making a big assumption without any evidence to support it – just like the young girl above.

I have spent a lot of time studying this area and I have learned techniques and tips to handle fears better. And I can see it having a hugely positive impact on my business.

> **Do you ever hear yourself say, "I do not have the experience to do that." or "That would never work for my business!" Be conscious of the assumptions you make in business and challenge them.**

82-Year-Old Granny Passes Her Driving Test

An 82-year-old granny from Wexford passed her driving test. She had tried and failed numerous times before. The media love this kind of story (great PR for the driving instructor too).

The thing that impressed me about this story was this woman's persistence. She had tried many times before and failed but she kept going. In my humble opinion, **persistence is the single most important quality we must have to succeed in business.**

I am sure people might be thinking, 'What about selling, marketing, etc.?' All those skills are important but they alone are useless without persistence.

Why are persistence and determination so important? Unfortunately, in business the odds are stacked against us. Most businesses won't succeed. The stats are frightening – I will not even go into them. Most things we try in business do not work. That is nobody's fault, it is just the way it is.

Look back at marketing campaigns you tried before and see how many worked.

I would guess for every ten things we try in business, maybe only two will work. Which is exactly why persistence is so very important.

If we keep trying, learn from our experience and try again, we are bound to be successful. I am sure you have heard this definition of insanity before: 'Doing the same thing over again and hoping for a different result.'

We must learn when things do not work and adjust our approach. Too many people quit and give up trying. Thomas Edison had over 10,000 attempts to invent the electric lightbulb before he eventually succeeded. He was quoted as saying, 'I ran out of ways that would not work.'

And I think business is the same. If we keep trying, tweaking our approach, learning and applying our new knowledge, we will have to succeed.

I believe persistence is the most important quality to have in business. It does not matter how many time you fail. If you learn from each experience and keep trying, you are bound to succeed.

The Most Dangerous Words in Business

As the old saying goes, "If I had a euro for every time I have heard those words – I would indeed be a rich man."

Why is the following response so dangerous?

"Yes, but my business is different."

Because it is normally uttered by a business person just after somebody has told him/her an idea that might help his/her business. Or it may be that the person is at a seminar where some new technology or method is being discussed. By uttering the words, 'Yes, but my business is different,' they are saying their mind is not open to learning new ideas.

Business is all about change and adapting to changing circumstances. If somebody is not open to new ideas and changing with the times, they will not survive in business. That is why those words are so dangerous.

Why do people say it? I think there are a couple of reasons. People are not thinking of the principles of good business. For example, if somebody is in the plant hire business and they hear of some new technology, they may mistakenly think that it does not apply to them.

Another reason people say 'Yes, but my business is different,' is that they are not open to new ideas.

If you find yourself saying those words, please also hear alarm bells.

Regardless of what your business does, the principles of business are the same for everybody. You have a product or service. You must make sales. Then you must ensure the customer is happy. More money should come in than go out, etc., etc., etc....

The principles of business do not change.

What prompted this message? I received a lovely message from a woman on my email list. Monica's business sells insurance to farmers in Boston.

'In the US, we are all 'Thankful' this week... which seems a rarity given the economic mess. Hope your emails bring you and your clients much to be thankful for! This note is just to say again how much we enjoy your daily emails here in the office. Monica.'

If my emails are relevant to Monica selling insurance to farmers in Boston then I think it proves my point.

**It does not matter what your business does.
Business is the same all over the world.
"Yes, but my business is different."
Do not utter these words – EVER!**

Why We Do the Things We Do

Every day around 3.30pm, Charles gets up from his desk, walks to the canteen, buys a chocolate chip cookie and eats it while chatting to work colleagues.

Charles had started to put on weight and his wife had passed a few comments. He decided to lose weight and wanted to cut out the mid-afternoon cookie. But he found it very difficult to change, which led him to study habits and how we can change them.

Why is it so hard to change our habits? Have you ever tried to lose weight or get fit? Have you ever joined a gym, went for a few weeks and never went back? Most of us have done that at some stage.

The cookie man above is called Charles Duhigg and his study on habits led to a fascinating book called 'The Power of Habit.' The book is well titled as habits can be very powerful.

95% of what we do every day are habits. There is a three-step loop in every habit and if we can study this and understand it, this can make changing habits easier. The three-step loop is: cue – routine – reward. In the example of Charles and the cookie, his three-step loop was:

1. Cue: around 3.30pm every afternoon, he felt the urge for a cookie.
2. Routine: his routine was walking to the canteen to buy a cookie.
3. Reward: eating the cookie and chatting with friends.

Charles had identified his three-step loop. How could he break this habit? Charles experimented with different rewards. Instead of buying the cookie, some days he went for a short walk and other times, he brought a candy bar with him and would eat it while chatting to a friend at his desk.

After a while Charles realised something. He got a bit bored mid-afternoon and craved some company for ten minutes – the craving was not for a cookie but for some company.

The next step is to isolate the cue – what is triggering the craving? Studies have found that cues fall into five categories – location, time, emotional state, other people and the immediately preceding action.

A typical day for Charles was like this:

Location: Sitting at his desk.

Time: 3.32pm emotional state – bored.

Other people: No-one.

The immediate preceding action: Just answered an email.

After doing this for several days, Charles isolated his cue – it was to have a cookie around 3.30pm in the afternoon.

Next up was a plan to break the habit. Charles decided that at 3.30pm every day, he would go a friend's desk and chat for ten minutes.

He set his alarm for 3.30pm and when it went off, he walked to a friend's desk and chatted for ten minutes. Other days, it did not work and he succumbed to a cookie. But after a while, he got into the habit of going to his friend's desk every day and he did not miss his cookie. After a few weeks, he hardly thought about the routine and he did not eat cookies anymore mid-afternoon. He had formed a new habit and did not need to think about it.

Obviously, this is covered in much more detail in the book, which I would highly recommend. And if you want to change any habit, why not follow the steps Charles followed above to get rid of his cookie habit, forever.

> **Habits follow a pattern of: Cue - routine - reward.**
> **If you become aware of your pattern, it can be easier to change habits.**

The Marshmallow Test

A four-year-old child is sitting in a room looking at a marshmallow. A man has just left the room. He has told the four-year-old they have a choice, eat the marshmallow now or wait until he comes back and get a second marshmallow.

This may seem a bit unfair on a four-year-old child. It is easy to imagine the four-year-old eating the marshmallow and not wanting to wait.

This test was conducted in the 1960s. And as you can imagine, many four-year-olds ate the marshmallow. But others did not. Some waited a short while and were rewarded with a second marshmallow.

This experiment was conducted in Columbia University by a professor, Walter Mischel. What he discovered was that some children could delay gratification.

Having the discipline to wait is an important personality trait. It has often been linked to success in later life.

Indeed, Professor Mischel followed up this test many years later. He found the children who could delay gratification were more successful in life in comparison to than those who had eaten the marshmallow straight away.

How do you think you would have responded if you faced the marshmallow test? I am sure we would all like to think that we would have waited but … As business owners, we all face our own marshmallow tests every day.

You are working on an important job and you hear the ping of an incoming email. What do you do? Eat the marshmallow (check your email) or wait? You may be working on a new product and the phone rings. Do you rush to pick it up? (maybe another marshmallow moment) or wait?

Two key characteristics of successful people are:

1. They know how to prioritise.
2. They have discipline to stick to that important job until it is done (no marshmallows here).

The next time you are tempted by an email, phone or prospect of going online… Why not think of that four-year-old child and **WAIT**.

> **Even though the study seemed a bit cruel, the four-year-old child who could delay gratification (eat the marshmallow), got a reward. The same applies to us in life.**

Why Doesn't Rocky Catch Rabbits (Excusitis)

Last week, I called to my sister's house to drop something off. There was nobody home. I went around the side gate to the back garden. Their Jack Russell dog, Rocky, was sitting by the back wall sunning himself. He looked up when I came around the corner of the house but did not budge. Normally, he would run over all excited when I called into the house.

I have always suspected his eyesight is not the best. I decided to walk towards him to see when he would respond. I was about six feet away from him before he recognised me and ran over all excited. This confirmed what we always suspected about Rocky – he is half blind.

You may recall from earlier mentions that Rocky's lack of prowess in the rabbit catching department was the source of much bemusement in our family. He had a long tradition to live up to from previous O'Brien dogs. Now at least we have some idea why he does not catch rabbits. He cannot see them. He has a good excuse. What is your excuse? (No, I do not mean for not catching rabbits!)

- Do you have a list of important things to do in your business?
- Maybe contact some past customers about repeat business?
- Or follow up on some recent prospect?
- Do something with your website or on social media?

Possible Excuses

➢ Something always gets in the way.
➢ You are too busy (that is the one I hear most often)
➢ Not enough hours in the day.

Somebody once coined a great saying for this… **excusitis.**

Do you suffer from excusitis?

There is always some reason why the important jobs do not get done. Many of my clients are good and crack on with stuff. But others do not get stuff done and then blame everybody else. They just stop short of 'the dog ate my homework' excuse. I have a low tolerance for excusitis. Be honest with yourself when that important job slips again.

How to get it done:
- Prioritise it.
- 80:20 it.
- Eat that frog.
- Just Do It (JDI).

No more excusitis.Rocky has a good excuse. What is yours?

> **Do you suffer from excusitis?**
> **Rocky is half blind and has a good reason for**
> **not catching rabbits.**
> **What is your excuse for not getting important jobs done?**

You Cannot Do It on Your Own

I like to keep fit and exercise a few mornings a week. It is such a great start to the day and I am normally buzzing with energy afterwards. Spinning, rowing and pilates are the main ones I do. I used to play five-a-side soccer. But I got slower and the young lads got quicker. I got sense and gave it up.

I am not sure if you have ever gone on the rowing machines in the gym. I have used them for years, badly I might add with knees and elbows flying everywhere. Then I learned the proper technique and it made all the difference. Rowing on your own is difficult. I got into the habit of rowing with a good friend of mine, John. Then he left the gym and I did very little rowing.

John re-joined the gym and we started rowing together again. I love the rowing. We do 2km or 5km. We track our time and must knock a few seconds off it every time.

The difference between rowing on your own or with somebody else is amazing. With somebody else you can get into a rhythm and row together. You have a focus to beat the last time you did. He reminds me of the right technique.

We encourage each other (especially important when the energy levels are low).

A few people commented to me that they have no-one to talk to in business. I am fortunate as I have a few good friends who know me and my business. We bounce ideas off each other on a regular basis. Talking to somebody else can give you a totally different view on an issue.

Recently I spoke to two friends about a certain issue. Amazingly they both gave me a similar answer. Since then I have changed direction in one area of my business and it is working very well. And remember it is a two-way street. I know my friends in business get a different insight when they talk to me about their business.

- Are you joined network groups?
- Do you have business neighbours you could talk with?
- What about customers/suppliers?

Do not be worried thinking 'they will not have time for that.' Everybody in business has stuff they need to talk about. Nobody can do it on their own.

Most successful people in business surround themselves with like-minded ones. Birds of a feather flock together. Make sure you pick your 'flock' carefully.

Cold Sweats Outside the Furniture Shop

There I was several years ago, sitting in my car outside a furniture shop. I had been persuaded by business friends that I needed to add walk-ins to my marketing mix. It was a nice sunny day but I barely even noticed. There is a good chance there were beads of cold sweat on my forehead. I had never done this before and I was not looking forward to it.

What if the owners were nasty to me? What if I became an incoherent mess when I tried telling them about my business? If things were going badly, I could just buy a three-piece suite!

Finally, I plucked up the courage and walked into the shop. There were a few customers walking around and I noticed three members of staff. I thought it would help to know the product. I spent five minutes walking around looking at the furniture. This relaxed me a bit.

After a while most of the customers had left the shop. I wandered up near the front. A woman in a suit, who looked like the owner/manager, asked me if I needed help. I said I was just browsing and we engaged in chit-chat about the weather. Then I asked her how business was doing.

She told me business was good but getting and keeping good staff was an issue. I told her a little bit about my marketing service and left a business card. I walked into another nearby business and had a nice chat with a manager. By the time I was walking into the fourth business, I was really enjoying myself and had a big beaming smile across my face.

This was partly relief as I had not been thrown out of any business.

There is an old saying, 'Do the thing you fear and the death of fear is certain.'

At that moment, I finally understood what that saying really meant. In my head, I had built up the worst possible scenarios before I did any walk-ins. And after doing them, I realised that I had nothing to fear.

I was reminded of this when I did some more walk-ins. Some of these were to people I know, while others were to 'cold' businesses who did not know me. I got at least one good meeting this week from two hours of walk-ins. As a marketing strategy, it is worth considering doing some bit of it. And even if it is not suitable for your sector, maybe a slightly different approach can be taken.

With one client who was targeting large manufacturers, we hand delivered a nice envelope with the prospects name on it and followed up with a phone call. This worked well as the hand-written delivered envelope was opened and read before those received in the post. Happy walk-ins.

My biggest fear was cold walk-ins and I conquered that by doing it. What is your biggest fear in business? Do the thing you fear and the death of fear is certain.

SECTION 5

FINANCE

Are Your Customers Toilet Trained?

This does qualify as one of the stranger questions I have asked. But please bear with me as I think you may appreciate why I am asking.

I had an interesting session with a new client. It was spent reviewing money owed to him and his payment terms. Quite a bit of my time these days is spent on sales and marketing. But those fifteen years working as an accountant still has its uses. And my job is to help my client where the need is greatest, (even if that sets back my timeline for becoming a fully signed up member of the recovered accountants club...).

As we reviewed money owed, it became clear that customers were allowed pick up bad habits, such as not paying for goods for three months, sometimes six months and even longer. Customers can only do this if they are allowed get away with it. And it is very common in Ireland.

Somebody half-jokingly said, that these customers had bad habits, a bit like not training your dog. And of course, they are spot on.

If you do not train your dog, he will pee and crap all over your floor. And if you do not train your customers, they will pee and crap all over you – by not paying you on time, by paying you six months after they got the goods, even after looking for discounts.

I know many businesses with similar problems. Maybe you are one of them. I have done a lot of work with businesses in this area over the years. And I have cleaned up a lot of crap.

How do you tackle this situation?

I believe my definition of a customer is a bit different from that of many others.

> **My definition of a customer: Someone who buys your product and pays you when you want to be paid (not when they decide).**

The critical words in that sentence are 'when you want to be paid.' What do you need to do? Set payment terms that determine when you want to be paid. And stick to them.

For example, with an IT hardware client, all clients must pay on delivery. They will get agreement in writing and verbally before delivering the PC's. We give you the products in exchange for a cheque.

Will some customers complain? Of course they will. Because they were given bad habits. Some people will be happy to accept these terms. And others won't.

It is always easier to set strict payment terms with new customers (like training puppies). Like when you are house-training a dog, do not let customers pee and crap all over you. Set strict payment terms. And find customers who are happy to pay you on those terms.

> **If a dog is not trained, it will pee and crap all over your kitchen. It is the same with customers who delay paying you for months.**
> **Take control of this situation from the start and decide when you want to be paid.**

This May Shock You

I hope you are sitting down as this may come as quite a shock to you. If yours is anything like many of those I have worked with in the past, you may have a large 'Profit Gap' in your business. If you have a service business, this is 100% applicable to you. And even if you have a product business it is still relevant as you are selling both materials and labour.

Let us say you have a service business like a web designer. You work by yourself and invoiced €40,000 last year. Your hourly charge out rate is €80.

Let us crunch some numbers...
Sales €40,000
Divided by 48 weeks = €833
Divided by €80 = 10.4 hours per week

Which means, on average, you worked 10.4 productive hours every week last year. What were you doing the rest of the time? How is this possible you may ask?

Not suggesting you were not working but those hours could have been spent on meetings with potential clients, travel, admin, marketing, etc. Of course, there was probably extra time spent on client jobs that you did not charge for.

Ok, let us crunch some more numbers and assume you worked three productive days per week (which does not seem unreasonable) ....

Productive hours (3 days x 8 hours) = 24
Multiplied by €80
Multiplied by 48 weeks
Sales €92,160
Your sales just went from €40,000 to €92,160, an increase of 230%. And if you have a service business and have a team of people working for you, the news is even better.

I have done this exercise for architects, engineers, accountants, solicitors and others and I always find 'lost' profit.

Here is how it goes:
Multiply the people by their hourly rate by 32 hours per week. A senior architect could be charged out at €80 per hour, which is €2,560 per week. Let us keep this simple and assume there are no junior staff at lower rates – just ten senior architects.

10 architects X 32 hours X €80/hour = €25,600

When I ask for their average weekly 'actual' sales, guess what the number comes in around? Sometimes it has been €21,000 but other times it has been as low as €12,250.

Which means that over 52 weeks, that architectural firm had sales of €637,000 when it should have been €1,331,200. They somehow 'lost' €694,200 of profit over the year. This figure seems incredible and hard to believe but I have seen these numbers come out like this on numerous occasions. This is not an isolated case.

You may well be thinking, 'How is this possible?' It is possible because these firms do not think this way (or grab a calculator like I do and see if their profits are going down the drain).

And if you own a product business and think, 'This does not apply to me,' think again. I found similar profit gaps of between €114,000 up to €417,000 in product businesses. This is all 'popping' out of my 80:20 analysis.

Over the six months working with them, I have helped my clients get some extraordinary results and helped them grow their profits significantly. And the amazing thing is, we were doing this without increasing sales volumes.

All this profit is 'hidden' within their existing customers. You just have to know where to look.

To see if your business has a profit gap, you need two pieces of information - your most recent profit & loss account and your standard method for setting your selling price.
Then compare the gross profit from your pricing method to the gross profit in your profit and loss account.

What You Really Think of Accountants

Thanks to all the people who replied to my survey to rate your accountant. There were some very interesting findings and I will share some of those with you now.

First up is your relationship with your accountant and how it can be improved, for both parties. Then there is the possibility of doing surveys in your own business. As you will see from the results below, it highlights areas where accountants can grow their income.

Here are the main findings:

Question 1: How do you rate your satisfaction level with your accountant?
The most popular responses were happy (56%) and mildly dissatisfied (28%).

I have heard that 1 in 4 people would leave their accountant and the 28% above tallies with this.

What would you think if you find out that 1 in 4 of your customers were somewhat unhappy with you? Personally, I would be horrified. It is a big % for any business.

Question 2: What areas were you did-satisfied with?
• Only see their accountant once or twice a year (78%)
• A feeling that they are small client and down their priority list (57%)
• Do not explain your accounts (36%)
• Use too much technical jargon (31%)

While the first one is a complaint, it is also a big opportunity. While many clients cannot afford higher fees, they cannot get a higher level of service; others can afford to see their accountant more often, maybe every two months.

When I mentioned this to a group of start-up businesses, they could not believe that most businesses only see their accountant once or twice a year. Maybe accountants have their model wrong and need to set it up so they see most of their clients every two or three months for a review. The accountant will get higher fees and the business gets better advice.

Question 3: If you were going to switch accountants, what would be the main reason?
While price was only 6%, service levels came in at 68%, again somewhat consistent with the earlier answers.

To summarise: if you are an accountant, you need to get talking to all your clients and maybe conduct your own survey. This can result in changes to the nature of your relationship with your client. It can also mean a happier client and more fees for you.

**If you are a business owner and you are not happy with your accountant, maybe you need to have chat and see what can be done to improve things.
And if you have not conducted a survey of your clients, maybe it is time to do so.**

Secretary of the Year
(How knowing your numbers can make all the difference)

Some time back I started working with a new client in the software industry. He had invested a lot of money in a new product and cash flow was tight. He needed to cut costs and beef up sales.

When I analysed his costs, one figure stood out like a sore thumb. I concluded he must have the 'Secretary of the Year' working for him. Why? Well, because she had received six pay increases in the previous eighteen months. She must have been some worker, right?

The only problem was that the owner did not know about the wage increases. The secretary paid the wages. She just decided to give herself a little bit extra… and then another little bit...

Shortly afterwards, she was moved on (and was fortunate not to end up in the courts). Of course, she could not have done this if the owner was not 'asleep at the wheel' of his business.

The first thing I insisted on was the owner signing all cheques from then on. I needed to put some simple reporting systems in place so this man would know what was going on in his business.

He was not financially minded so I developed a simple spread sheet for him. This report listed the cash in and cash out on a weekly basis. It was cumulative: he could see on a weekly, monthly and annual basis. We had another spread sheet that listed sales and money owed to the business. A third report showed weekly purchases and money owed to suppliers.

He was amazed at the difference these simple reports made to his business.

He now could see his weekly and monthly running costs. Within four weeks, we cut running costs by 20%. He could see cash in and sales. For the first time ever, he felt in control of his business. With that in place, my next job was to get him out of the office and selling.

This story illustrates the importance of knowing the numbers in your business. Without these reports, I believe the business would have run out of money within six weeks and it may have folded. Sadly, the owner would not have realised this until it was too late.

When I run training courses, I have lots of stories like these to illustrate the importance of knowing your numbers. It can be the difference between your business making it or not.

- So, do you know your key numbers?
- What are your monthly running costs?
- What is your monthly break-even figure?

Knowing these and other key numbers could be the most important thing you do in your business this year.

> **Not knowing your numbers in business is like watching a sports match with no scoreboard.**

What Are Your Break-Even Sales?

Your break-even sales is the minimum you need to do every week. This figure means your total sales equals your total costs. Ideally in business, we need to make a profit. I encourage clients to calculate their break-even sales… and then add on a figure for profit.

This break-even note was prompted by an email I received. *'Can you do an email on working to a daily break-even point? The figure you must get to each day to know that from then on you are making money. Very relevant I think!'*

This email came from Bobby who deals with lots of food companies.

There is no way of doing this without using numbers. I will try to explain it without boring the pants off you…

Let us assume Jim makes chairs. He sells these chairs for €100 each. The steel and plastic needed to make each chair costs €40.

Jim's has other monthly costs like wages, insurance, phones, etc. (overheads). These overhead costs total €5,000 per month.

What is Jim's daily break-even?

How many chairs does he have to sell every day just to cover his costs?

The easiest thing is to calculate his break-even sales by month first. Then we can easily work out his daily break-even sales. The first thing we must work out is Jim's gross margin %

We work out his gross margin like this:
Sales minus direct cost = gross profit
Gross profit divided by sales = gross margin %

Taking Jim's figures above this would look like:
Sales €100 minus direct cost €40 = gross profit €60
Gross margin % = 60%

Now we divide Jim's overhead costs by his gross margin %
Overheads €5,000
Gross margin 60%
Break-even sales = €8,333

Just to double check this figure.
Assume Jim's monthly sales are €8,333. We know that his steel and plastic cost is 40% of this, that is €3,333. His other overhead costs are €5,000
Sales €8,333 minus direct costs €3,333 minus overheads €5,000 = 0
Jim's monthly break-even sales figure is €8,333

If we assume twenty working days in a month, his daily break-even figure is €8,333 divided by twenty, that is €417 per day. The chair sells for €100; he must sell 5 chairs per day to break-even.

But we are not in business to just break-even – we need to make a decent profit. I would advise Jim to sell 7, 8, 9 or more chairs per day. He can take his pick. A figure like this can provide huge focus for a business. If Jim only sold 3 chairs in a day, he knows he has lost money.

Would it be helpful to know your daily break-even figure?

Or even your weekly/monthly break-even figure. All the figures needed to calculate your break-even sales, just like above, should be available from your most recent set of accounts. And do not forget to add on a profit element to your break-even figure. In business, it is key to know your break-even sales figure. It is the minimum sales you need to have so that you pay all your costs that month and have nothing left. Obviously, the point of business is to make a profit. You can take your break-even sales figure and add on your required profit. When a business is struggling, hitting the break-even may be the initial target. Even successful businesses can have seasonal peaks and troughs and it is important to hit a minimum of break-even in those quieter months.

> **Your break-even sales figure is one of the most important for you to know. Jim needs to sell 5 chairs per day to break-even.**
> **What do you need to do in your business every day to hit your break-even sales figure?**

Sales Are Vanity, Profit Is Sanity

You probably have heard that one before but it is one of my favourites. I can still hear some wise old clients who have said it to me. I have seen many business people make the mistake of focusing on sales only. Their sales could be growing at 20% but their costs are increasing by 30%. And even though they are busier, the business is worse off.

How is this possible? People are so busy with new customers, they do not notice that costs have gone out of control. Or they may not notice that the profit margin on the new orders is too low.

Do you have a 'scoreboard' in your business tracking all the key figures every week? That way you can tell if you are just making sales or making profit.

If you work hard getting sales of €5,000 but your costs are also €5,000 then you have nothing to show for your hard work. And that is where the saying came from: *sales are vanity, profit is sanity*.

The real purpose of business is not to make a sale – it is to make a profitable sale.

If the sale is €5,000 your total costs should be €3,000 or €3,500 or €4,000. But not €5,000, or heaven forbid €6,000. Believe me, it happens all the time.

How can you prevent this happening to you? You need to have a sales target you keep a close eye on. And this sales target must include your running costs, a wage for you and a profit.

Let us assume all these add up to €10,000 per month. Then

you keep a close eye on your actual figures so you know if you are in line to hit your sales target. Every day and every week as you progress through the month, track your sales. And make sure that you hit your sales target.

> **Keep 'sane' by making profits as well as sales. Business is not about making a sale, as most business owners think. It is all about making a profitable sale.**

Business Lessons from A Tight Pants

Do you know that feeling? You're getting dressed in the morning, and your pants feels tighter than usual. Has somebody robbed my pants? Did it shrink in the wash?

And then reality hits. You've put on weight. It is not a nice feeling, is it? "I was only on holidays for a week. I know I had a few glasses of wine and some chocolate biscuits but…".

Even though it is not a nice feeling, it is a good thing. I have left the gym slip in recent weeks as it often does in summer time, and have been doing an extra bit of socialising recently. The tight pants is like a wake-up call. I am going back to the gym tomorrow. And I have dusted the cobwebs off the juicer. What's the business equivalent of the 'tight pants'?

If you're not 100% sure, these may be tell-tale signs:
- Your bank balance is slipping.
- Your lodgements or value of invoices raised drops.
- Fewer orders.

What can you do about it?

What is your business equivalent of 'going to the gym'?
It is not rocket science. Get on the phone or get out there and find more customers and sales. Adapt the 4-mula formulae to grow sales. 4-mula is doing four different things to get sales every day. It could be send 4 emails, phone 4 clients, follow up 4 quotations, etc.

If things go slack for me, I will do some or all the following:
- Phone and meet with customers from twelve months ago.
- Ask customers for referrals.
- Contact businesses who have passed me business before.
- Follow up some recent quotation.
- Conduct an online survey and follow up responses.

> **You need to have early warning systems in your business to tell you if things are going off track (like the tight pants feeling).**

SECTION 6

SALES AND CUSTOMER SERVICE

Lessons from The Window Cleaner

A window cleaner knocked on my door one day. Being a window cleaner he asked me, "Would you like your windows cleaned?" Not knowing who he was, I politely declined. He replied that he was in the area regularly and named a few people whose windows he cleaned. I knew one of the people he named, so I could feel my resistance dropping. He seemed a very polite chap and he was gently persistent.

Then he said, "It is only €10 for the outside and we'll be finished in a jiffy." I was thinking those windows could do with a clean, so eventually I said, "Ok."

True to his word he cleaned the windows quickly (helps that I live in a bungalow). When I was paying him, he introduced himself as Simon, told me he would be back around in six weeks and if I wanted to give him my number, he would phone me the day before. I gave him my number thinking I would never hear from him again.

About six weeks later, I got a call from Simon saying he was in the area tomorrow and would I like my windows cleaned. I said "sure but I'm out all day tomorrow". "No problem", he said. If I wanted to leave the money under a bin, he could collect it and clean my windows.

I did and Simon cleaned my windows. And he continued to do so for years. Now I was very impressed with the simplicity and effectiveness of Simon's approach.

There are good lessons here for us business owners.

How often do we sell to somebody once and not think about the repeat sale?

How many times do you contact past customers for repeat business?

Simon made it very easy for me to buy from him again. He took my number. He rang back six weeks later. And even though I was not there, he made it easy for me to pay him.

Encouraging repeat business is one of the core marketing principles that I go through with all my clients. Remember Simon's approach and get more repeat business from your existing customers. Go for the low hanging fruit of repeat sales.

How can you make it easy for your customers to buy from you again?

Simon took my number and rang me six weeks later when he was in the neighbourhood. Many people in Simon's situation would have left their business card with me and waited for me to phone them, which would probably never have happened. Simon got repeat sales because he took control of the situation.

They say it is six times easier to sell to an existing customer than to find a new one. Do you make it easy for customers to buy again?

Excuse Me, Do You Have A Moment?

Asking permission is very important. Especially if you are phoning people near dinner time, when the calls are often from somebody asking if you're happy with your current phone provider!

Let us back up a small bit. I am going to share a story with you. It is also one of the most successful selling tactics you can employ in business. And while this story is about a shop, this is applicable to every type of business.

I was doing some work with a shop which sold timber floors. If somebody asks me to help increase their sales, I need to understand their sales figures. I get them to measure certain figures, like conversion rate.

For every 100 people who come into the shop, how many buy? Before I tell you, take a guess. For them it was 20%. That is not unusual. For every 100 people who came into their shop, eighty did not buy. Now you will never get 100% but if this shop converted another 10%, it would add 50% to their sales.

I suggested taking people's details and if they did not come back and buy within a week, phone them back and see if you can encourage them back into the store to buy from you.

"You can't do that!" I was told by the owner.

"Why not?" I asked.

"Nobody else does it," he said. I hear this all the time...

So I heard myself saying, "Give me the quotation book and I will do it."

"Ok," said the owner.

This happened in my first six months in business and even though I heard follow ups worked really well, I had never done it myself.

So that evening about seven o'clock, I was sitting nervously in front of my phone. "Hi, this is Neil from X flooring shop. You were in with us recently looking at a maple hardwood floor... Do you have a few minutes to talk?" And surprise, surprise, they did. Nobody attacked me or told me to get lost.

What I discovered after ten calls is that people fell into three categories:

1. They had bought somewhere else. (This is a great opportunity to find out why.)

2. The house is not ready. (Arrange to call back at a later date.)

3. They have shopped around, are ready to buy but can't decide where.

This third category are the ones you really want short term. What can you say or do to entice them back to you? There is a good chance you are the only ones to phone them back, and that is a big plus. I could give you pages and pages of examples of how beneficial this has been for businesses of all shapes and sizes over the years.

One bathroom shop phoned a woman who had been in two months earlier and within days she came back and spent over €10,000.

Do you follow up with people who contact you and do not buy? Do you get their details and follow up with a phone call or email?

Believe me, if you do this, you will increase your sales.

A prospect or lead who does not buy on the first day, is the closest thing you have to a customer. Along with spending time and money chasing after new prospects, divert a little bit towards following up prospects and your business will reap the rewards.

> **The closest thing you have to a customer is a prospect you have spoken to already. Make sure you follow up everybody who has not bought and watch your sales grow.**

Business Lessons from McDonald's

What happens if you walk into McDonald's and order a burger? Ok, it used to be "Do you want fries with that?" but not anymore. This is how it works now...

Customer: "Can I have a quarter pounder?"

Staff member: "Certainly, madam/sir, is that a quarter pounder meal?"

Customer: "Ah – yes." (They may have been caught off guard and say yes.)

Staff member: "Is that a medium meal or large meal?"

Customer: "Aah – large?" (Caught off guard, so they say the last one mentioned.)

Not sure what your experience of McDonald's has been to date, but even if you have a healthy diet, it is difficult to avoid going there occasionally. And it is probably impossible, if you have kids.

What just happened above? The sale of €3.50 has been increased to €7.00. It has just doubled.

How did that happen? The staff member asked two 'upsell' questions.

We know not everybody will say yes. But enough people do to make it worthwhile (I will have some numbers for you in a moment).

Why am I telling you this?

This is a great lesson in increasing average sales. Nobody does it better than McDonald's.

I often use this example when I run a training course and am discussing one of the easiest ways to increase sales. Selling more items to your existing customer is one of the 'low hanging fruits' in increasing sales. Why? Because these customers are coming to you already. You do not have to do anything to get them. You just need to have other products to sell them. And if you only sell one product, you need to develop more.

Here are the numbers I promised you. These are a bit old but still make the point.

Every day in the U.S., twenty-five million people go to a McDonald's.

When asked, "Do you want fries?" three out of ten people say "Yes."

The fries are $1 each.

That is 365 days per year.

Extra sales = 25 Million x (3 divided by 10) x 365 x $1.

That is a lot of extra sales and all from asking your customers one question.

So, what is your McDonald's question?

When your customer is buying from you, what can you ask them to upsell and increase your average sale? How can you systemise that question so it is asked every time? This is not rocket science. As Nike say, *'Just Do It.'*

The six most profitable words in history used by McDonald's and which can double the average sale are "Do you want fries with that?"
What is your McDonald's question?

The Hammer and The Glass

Many years ago, a salesman was travelling to hardware stores selling his new style glass. This new glass was unbreakable and everybody thought sales would take off. But it did not happen. The salesman was getting desperate so one day he tried something different. He went into a hardware store, found the owner and asked him to hold the glass in front of himself, at waist height. He got a hammer, walked up to the owner and hit the glass hard with the hammer. To the owner's astonishment, the glass did not break. He immediately ordered two dozen.

The salesman employed the same tactic and his sales figures soared. He was the talk of the whole district. Before too long before his company's competition brought out a similar glass.

His sales technique was so successful that all their sales people employed the same tactic with the hammer and the glass.

His sales dropped back down again. He thought about it for a little while and decided on a different approach. He went into a hardware store with his glass, holding it in front of himself at waist height. He asked the owner to get a hammer and hit the glass hard with the hammer. To the owner's astonishment, the glass did not break. He immediately ordered two dozen.

The message of this story is simple: in sales situation 'show, do not tell.' Rather than trying to explain your product, show the prospect.

- Can you do a demo?
- Do you have a before and after?
- What are the tangible benefits of using your service?

Also have some strong testimonials from satisfied clients. Tell stories, especially around your most common objection, and how somebody had concerns before they purchased but after they used the product, they were delighted.

We have all been in a sales situation where the salesperson was trying to sell the product just by talking and we could see the prospect's eyes glaze over (no pun intended).

Make sure your prospect's eyes are not glazing over and 'show, do not tell.'To 'show, do not tell', can you do a demo, have a video, client testimonials, etc.?

Right Under Your Nose

I was working with a client when his business partner came back after being out all day. Let us call him John. While his partner was out of the office for a few minutes, I started chatting to John about his day. He came back to the office with €30,000 worth of orders. Not a bad day's work.

Our conversation went something like this...

"How did you get those orders?" I asked.

"I know these clients, so I called to the site and met the manager for a coffee," replied John.

"They didn't contact you or say they had a job?" I said.

"No, it was on spec but after the coffee we walked around the site and one of the foremen stopped me and told me they have a job for me. And a few minutes later, the quality manager asked me to price something. As I walked around the site, I spotted a few areas where work was needed and I spoke to the section head, who told me to quote for the work," explained John.

"How often do you go on-site like this?" I asked curiously.

"Not often enough. Maybe once a month and I always come back with orders," John said.

"You must have about twenty similar sized clients, haven't you? How much business would you get if you spent one day per week calling to clients?" I asked.

"Loads more," agreed John.

"It is great you get all this work but I'm curious – why does it happen like that?"

"Two things – out of sight is out of mind, plus when I walk around the site, I can see things that need to be sorted," he said.

I have had similar conversations with so many clients over the years. We can put lots of time and effort into chasing new clients and new things, when there are loads of extra sales right under our nose.

Putting time and effort into talking to and meeting our existing clients always pays off with extra sales.

And even better when we target our 80:20 most profitable clients. Even if you can't call into the site like this, what could you do in the next week to make contact with existing or past clients? Make a phone call and arrange to visit them or meet up for a coffee? Send them a 'Thank you' card and follow up with a phone call/visit. I can almost guarantee that if you contact five clients in the next week, you will get extra sales from it.

What's your excuse for not doing it? Too busy?

You must NEVER be too busy for this type of activity.

So why not pick up your diary right now and block off half a day next week to contact/meet your customers.

> **Put time into meeting, chatting with current and past customers and you will see the rewards. You must never be too busy to do this.**

My Confession

I am lazy. There, it is said. It is out in the open. I have wanted to admit that for ages. But to me being lazy in business has its advantages. I want to find the easiest quickest cheapest way to grow sales. That is the approach I take with my own clients. And the approach I take myself. It reminds me of what Tim Ferris says in his great book, *'The 4-Hour Work Week.'* According to him: **'Being busy is a form of laziness – lazy thinking and indiscriminate action.'**

You cannot argue with that.

I was chatting with a colleague during the week. He is in the insurance business. He was telling me about the work they are doing on marketing. They have revamped their website and set up a database, all good stuff. But there was one idea screaming at me for his business. I know, as I have worked with insurance people before.

Taking my lazy approach, I want to find the easiest, quickest way to grow sales. For me it is cross selling. Sell more policies to their existing clients. This is the way I look at that business. There is a good chance this applies to you too.

Let us say the insurance business have 1,000 customers. Imagine a report that lists the 1,000 customers down the left-hand side. Now imagine they have ten products listed across the top of the page.

The average customer has two policies.

1,000 x 2 = 2,000 policies.

The maximum total number of policies is 1,000 x10 = 10,000 policies.

Okay, you will never get that number. But what if they cross sell and get one extra policy per customer. That would add 50% to their sales. Even if they got one extra policy for every second customer, that would add 25% to their sales.

Let us say the first customer has two policies: house insurance and car insurance. But they do not have their public liability insurance or their professional indemnity. Cross sell to existing customers is the easiest way for them to increase sales.

What about your business?

Do you cross sell to your customers?

How much extra sales would you get by cross selling?

I am all in favour of the easiest, quickest way to grow sales and more importantly, profits.

The easiest way to do this is to sell more to your existing customers. Better still is to sell more of your most profitable products to your best customers (whales).

Selling Lessons from Hare Krishna

Picture the scene…

A businessman is walking quickly through a crowded airport. He has a flight to catch. Would you think this is a good prospect to stop and look for a charitable donation? Most people would think not. Well, wait and see what happens next.

A woman approaches him and hands him a flower. The man, reacting with surprise, takes it. Almost immediately he tries to hand it back. The Hare Krishna member says it is a gift from them and it is his to keep, a donation to further the society's good works would be appreciated. The businessman tries to hand back the flower again.

"It's our gift to you," the woman responds.

There is visible conflict in the man's face. Should he keep the flower and walk away without giving anything or should he give a donation. With a nod of resignation, he fishes in his pocket for some notes and hand them over. The woman thanks him and he walks away. At the first rubbish bin he sees, he quickly disposes of his 'gift.'

What has just happened? Why does a busy businessman take a flower he clearly does not want? And then hands over money, only to throw away his gift at the first opportunity? The man has been subjected to one of the most powerful laws in the universe. It is called the Law of Reciprocation.

If somebody gives us something, we feel obliged to pay them back.

This is a story from a great book called, '*Influence – The Psychology Of Persuasion*' by Robert Cialdini.

Even if the gift is something we do not want, the Hare Krishna know this and use it very effectively to extract lots of money from people. Look at the reaction of the businessman. He clearly did not want the flower. But once he accepted it, he felt obliged to pay back the person, in this case, with a donation.

What does this mean to you in business?

Well lots of business people out there use this principle every day.

Ever been offered a free cheese sample in the supermarket? Ever receive a bundle of charity cards at Christmas with a soft message saying if you would like to keep the cards, you can make a donation of your choice to the charity? Think about ways you can use this in your business.

If you give a gift to your customers, many will feel obliged to pay you back. This gift does not have to be a product, it could be a small service.

We make decisions in a split second and reciprocation is one of these. If you do something for somebody, they will feel obliged to do something back.

Sales Lessons from the Boy Scouts

A man is walking down a street when he's approached by a twelve-year-old boy scout. "We're raising funds for our scout group and we have a circus on Saturday evening. The tickets are €5 each. Would you be interested in taking one?"

"No thanks," said the man.

"If you do not feel like taking a ticket, how about buying our chocolate bars? They are only €1 each..." asked the boy scout. The man bought two bars, even though he does not like chocolate. Later the man was trying to figure out what happened.

This story is also from Cialdini's book, '*Influence.*'

There are two factors at play here.

The first one is reciprocation. When the boy scout backs off his first request to buy a €5 ticket, this is seen as a concession. Human nature being what it is, if somebody gives us a concession, we feel obliged to give one back. The man felt obliged to buy the chocolate bars, even though he does not like them.

The second factor at work is contrast. The circus ticket is €5 and the chocolate bar is only €1. €1 seems much lower than €5.

By asking for the €5 sale first, being refused and then asking for the €1 sale, the boy scout had a much better chance of getting the sale than if he just asked for the €1 sale.

These two principles are part of human psychology – reciprocation and contrast. It is how we think and how we behave. I am not saying everybody responds this way, every time. But most of us respond that way, most of the time. Businesses use these approaches every day – car dealers, clothes shops and many others.

> **When telling customers your price range, start high, work down and you will increase your sales.**
> **Show me a product for €100 and the next one**
> **I see for €50 will seem cheap.**

Beef or Salmon

Beef or salmon is a common choice at weddings. It was also the name of a famous race horse. It is nice to have a choice especially for people who do not like seafood. We were on holidays one year in Kerry, staying near the sea. One evening we headed off to a highly-recommended seafood restaurant.

However, we were only in there less than two minutes. Why? Because they only served seafood. Some of our party do not eat seafood, making it an easy decision to leave. So, we travelled to another seafood restaurant a mile away. They had a selection of seafood, plus steak and chicken. Everybody was happy. We walked out of the first restaurant with €200 in our pocket and gave it to the second one.

Now one of the real benefits of being in business is that we can decide what kind of business to run, what kind of products we have, who we sell to, what price to charge. We may get some or all of these things wrong, which may or may not prove fatal to our business, yet still these decisions are ours to make.

In one way, I admire the first restaurant for picking their narrow niche. However, a greater part of me is slightly upset when I think of the amount of money that walks out the door of that business every day and walks in somewhere else because of an objection that is easy to fix.

In business, at some stage we all have to sell to a potential customer. Getting and handling objections is something most of us have to do.

A potential customer may say: "I have to think about it." "You are too expensive." "I must talk to my partner, dog, goldfish…"

These objections can be difficult to overcome and some sales will be lost. Like the example I gave earlier, if somebody does not like seafood, and that is all the restaurant serves, then nothing could be done about it.

If I was mentoring this business, I would ask them to track these walk outs for a week, estimate the average cover sales value, multiply it up and annualise the sales that are walking out the door.

What is the most common objection you get in your sales process? How do you handle it?

One great tip to improve conversion rate and sales is to list your top five objections and come up with a response for each one. Then learn them. Because when a potential client throws you an objection, your response must roll off your tongue. Throw the 'hot potato' back into their lap. Or the sale will be lost.

In every sales situation, you are likely to get objections. Be prepared for objections, have your response ready and toss the 'hot potato' back in the customer's lap.

The Jelly Effect

A man walks into a network event. He gets chatting to a woman he never met before and she asks him what he does.

"We design websites for businesses. This gives them a really good presence on the Internet. Our sites are easy to maintain and you can update them yourself. We're in this business fifteen years so we really know our stuff. It is mostly WordPress we work with," he told her.

"Are there any particular sectors you work with?" asked the woman.

"We work with everyone and anyone," said the man.

Across town a woman walked into a different network meeting. She got chatting to a man she never met before and he asked her what she does.

"We produce websites which give businesses a new online shop window to help grow their sales," she replied.

"That's sounds fascinating. Tell me more," he asked.

"Some recent clients we worked were jewellers, hotels, kitchen shops, wedding photographers, architects and many more. People come to us when their sales have been down in recent years and their cash flow is under pressure. After their website is built, their sales increase and the pressure on the cash flow eases," she explains.

"How do your websites increase their sales like that?" asked the man.

"We worked with a kitchen shop recently and they were desperate to get the sales back up. We redesigned their website and got them near the top of Google's rankings. We built a

172

new enquiry form on their site to capture people's details. This brought in an average of three strong enquiries per week and at least one of those people bought. Their average sale is €10,000. Our website has helped them add €500,000 in sales per year," the woman explained.

"That's amazing! We need you. Here's my card. Give me a call next week," said the man.

The second approach I picked up from an amazing little book called '*The Jelly Effect*' by Andy Bounds. It is a very good book that covers networking, how to be effective in sales meetings and giving good presentations. It is jam-packed with practical tips and pointers. Andy is one of the most effective communicators I have ever come across.

The name of the book comes from the notion of somebody walking up and throwing a bucket of jelly at you. Not very pleasant, the jelly will run off you and none will stick. The man in the first scenario jellies the woman. All he talks about is his business and their features. None of his message will stick. The woman at the second meeting is totally focused on her clients and the benefits they get from using her services.

Which of these two people are you most likely to remember?

If you wanted a website, who would you choose?

If you attend network meetings are you more like the man or the woman?

My advice is to learn the 'jelly' approach from this book and use it every time you meet anybody who can pass you a referral. Use it at any network event. Use it every time you are selling to someone.

> **People have a problem and they want your solution to fix it, so that after you are done, the problem is gone. Ask your prospect questions to identify their 'afters' and relate everything you say to these afters.**

The Real Reason the Titanic Left Cobh

Cobh is a hugely popular historic town. It was the final port the Titanic sailed from on its ill-fated maiden voyage. And after spending a Saturday morning trying to get some breakfast there, I think I know why it left... To get some decent grub!

My friend lives locally. One Friday evening we played golf, then we had a beautiful meal and a few drinks. We set off at 11am the next morning to grab some breakfast. One particular café had a good name. We grabbed a couple of seats there and waited. And we waited.

We were there fifteen minutes and in that time, nobody acknowledged we existed. Nobody came with a menu. Staff walked past us all the time. The owner was behind the counter. There were a dozen people in there and three staff members. Eventually from sheer frustration and growing hunger we left.

The second place we tried had a large number of tourists milling around. The café downstairs was closed. We asked some of shop staff about the café. It opened whenever the owner showed up.

On we went with our search. My friend was getting a bit embarrassed. It shouldn't be this hard to get a bit of breakfast in this town. Next place we tried seemed more promising.

"Do you serve a cooked breakfast?" we asked hopefully.

"Yes – hot scones and coffee," was the reply.

Not the hot breakfast we had in mind. Not saying there is no decent grub available on a Saturday morning in Cobh. But if there is, they keep it well hidden. On and on we went getting hungrier and more despairing as we went. We tried two more places before settling for our hot breakfast of.... coffee and scones.

As we sat looking out the window, there were hundreds of tourists milling around. If the locals could not find a decent breakfast they had no chance. What an opportunity this town is missing.

There are opportunities everywhere if you just open your eyes.

Unfortunately, the customer service in many Irish businesses leaves a lot to be desired. Not saying every place is as bad at the first one that left us waiting fifteen minutes. But many are not too far away from this.

Why is the customer service so bad?

I put it down to bad training and lack of procedures. As we sat looking out the window, we saw four tourists sitting down at a table outside our café. Ten minutes later, they are still sitting there and no staff member had approached them.

Regardless of what business you are in, there are opportunities to do better. Look at your competition and make sure you are better than them.

> **Most of your competition are so poor that with a bit of effort, you can do much better. Provide outstanding service and you will have a successful business.**

Lemon Wedges, Me A***

Now the waiter didn't exactly come out and say that but the look said it all. They say that 70% of communication in non-verbal.

We were out for a meal on a Friday night and we ordered fish for our main course. The lemon wedges were tiny so we asked the waiter if we could have some more. He did not say anything but the look said it all. He said nothing but you just knew what was going through his head. Not what you want when you go out for a drink and a meal at the end of a long week. In my mind, a restaurant is not just selling food, it is also selling service and an experience.

This is just a snippet of our experience as we went for a drink first in the bar and then for a three-course meal. With just one exception, the service was either basic or poor. And while the food was first class, the service was poor and we were both agreed at the end that we would not go back again by choice.

My sister, Edel, and myself discussed if we were being a bit harsh but I do not think so. The nature of these visits is that we report back what we experience and it is up to the owner to decide how to react. We will report back to my client in the next few days and I do not think he will be pleased.

If it was your restaurant, would you prefer to know this or

not? We will follow up with feedback to staff on our experience, give them some customer service training and send somebody else there for another 'mystery visit' in the next month.

Since that Friday night, I thought about customer service and what makes for a good experience or a bad one. I think the key is to make the customer feel a bit special, go the extra mile and do something they were not expecting. Make them want to come and buy from you again. Make it memorable.

I know these may sound like clichés and we have heard them all before but my experience on that Friday convinced me that they are 100% true. Even if you do not own a restaurant, how would your business do if a mystery customer visit was conducted?

There are ways of asking customers and doing surveys to find out what it is like when they deal with your business.

- Ask them.
- Better still, get a third party to ask them.
- Conduct an online survey.

Anytime I have carried out a survey for a business, it has given them feedback and information that was valuable to them. And by taking that information and making changes, you can improve your business. It is an exercise that needs to be done on a regular basis. Rinse and repeat.

When you make your customer feel special they will want to come back again.

You Know Where You Can Put Your Crème Brûlée

Every morning at around 11am Ken leaves his restaurant and walks to the local market to buy his fresh food supplies for that evening. He selects the finest monkfish from Mick Murphy's stall, as he knows Mick was up at 4.30am that morning and drove a four-hour round trip to have the freshest fish in Cork City. Ken knows the importance of the fresh good quality ingredients in the restaurant business.

His restaurant had won numerous awards in three years of business, including the best restaurant in the province and being one of Ireland's top 100 restaurants. One of the reasons that Ken knows the importance of good food was his excellent training and his experience working in some of the top restaurants in Paris, London and Dublin.

Although his restaurant had won numerous awards it was still one of Cork's best-known secrets. They asked me to help them with their marketing. During our weekly meetings, one comment stuck in my mind and as it was repeated several times, I asked the owners to elaborate. They said that many customers who had previously been regular visitors to the restaurant had stopped booking.

I suggested phoning some of these customers and conducting a survey to get feedback, to ascertain if there was any particular reason, why these people had stopped using the restaurant.

The feedback on the food was excellent. However, on the

service side the comments were not as complimentary. When I showed them the feedback they immediately pinpointed the culprit. One of the waitresses had caused problems in the past but they had given her a second chance. They spoke to the waitress and the whole thing came to a head the following weekend, when she told one customer where to put his crème brûlée!

She was fired and a replacement was hired and trained. The atmosphere and service immediately improved.

My clients had learned a hugely valuable lesson. Although they had trained extremely hard to provide the food and won numerous awards, one of their staff was undoing all the good work and was literally driving their customers away.

Lesson 1: Feedback from customers is vital and will often highlight areas that are having a negative impact on the business and need to be addressed.

Lesson 2: People are not your most important asset. The right people are your most important asset. The wrong people are a liability.

Lesson 3: If you have a people problem, deal with it. It is not going to go away by itself, and it will come back to bite you in the butt.

Do you know how customers feel about your business? If not, maybe it is time to find out.

Read Your Customer's Mind

A man walked into a business and tried hard to sell his blue widget. The company did not buy any widgets. A while later he discovered, by chance, the company had only wanted red widgets. The man thought long and hard about his business. He spent sleepless nights wondering what he could do to grow sales.

A while later he launched a marketing campaign for yellow widgets with pink dots. It was a huge success and he had record sales that month. The company who refused him earlier bought a dozen yellow widgets with pink dots.

- How did he know what they wanted?
- Did he read their minds?
- Was he a visionary for his industry?

No, he used an ingenious method that anyone else could have used. It has been used by businesses for a long time. He actually asked his customers and prospects what they wanted. He met them face to face and asked lots of questions. He conducted online surveys. He gathered together all the information from this research. He took this information on what his customers and prospects wanted. And he used it to design a marketing campaign. He used this information when he was in sales meetings.

It is easy to give people what they want when they have told you what they want. It is much harder to give them what they want when you're guessing.

I too have been using online surveys similar to widget-man. I have been doing this for both clients and for myself. With clients, I have taken the information gathered in the surveys and used it to market back to those same people. Like widget-man, if they tell me they want yellow widgets, I talk to them about our new yellow widget.

It is starting to work very well. I am using this approach more and more and plan to keep doing so. It is so logical, I do not know why I have not done more of it before now.

Do you think this approach might work for you to ask customers and prospects what do they want. And to turn around a short while later and say, "By the way, do you realise that we do…"

Do not be like widget-man trying to sell a blue product when the customer wants red. Take the guess work out of it.

Ask your customer what they want. It is hugely effective and provides great focus for marketing. Then provide that for them.

SECTION 7

GENERAL BUSINESS TOPICS

50 Shades Of Fog

I have taken up hill-walking in the last two years. And I love it. Lots of fresh air, stunning scenery and good company. Some days are bright and sunny. And others are wet and foggy. A bit like life. You know what Forrest Gump said about the box of chocolates…

One day in particular sticks in my mind… The day started out ok, but got worse as we ascended. As we got to the top of the mountain, a fog came in and you could barely see thirty yards in front of you. It could be a scary situation but we had the two essentials needed for that situation: a GPS compass and an experienced leader.

I was walking near the leader at one stage and I asked him how he was navigating. He showed me the compass, the map and explained how he was guiding us. We were walking in a big loop to the top of the mountain and back around to where we started. There were also markings and landmarks as we proceeded.

After talking to John, the leader, I summarised his approach as follows: we knew where we were and where we wanted to finish (back where we started). John's only focus was the next point.

He did not need to know every point along the way.

He would take us from point A to point B.

And then from point B to point C.

This reminded me of the story of how people crossed hundreds of miles of the Sahara Desert in a jeep. They got big plastic drums, painted them in bright colours and placed the drums at five mile intervals. When you started, you saw the first drum and headed towards it and when you got there you saw the next one and that was your sole focus. Taking it one step at a time and you could cross hundreds of miles of desert to your destination.

In business, it is pretty similar to our walk in the fog. You need to know your starting point and where you are going. You do not need to know every step of the way. You just need to know your next step and focus all your energy on getting there. People often procrastinate as they think they must know every step of the way before they start.

That is not the case. The hardest thing is make a start. Even if you make a mistake, it is much easier to change direction once you are going. Just focus on your next step and put all your energy into getting there.

> **You do not have to know every step of your business journey. You just need to know your final destination and the next stop on the way there.**

Do Bears Really S*** in the Woods?

Well as you will see in the following case, this particular bear is more interested in getting his dinner. Picture this scenario…

Two men are being chased by a bear in the woods. One of them stops to change into a pair of runners. The second man stops and looking down at the first man says, "Why are you changing into runners? You will never outrun that bear!" The first man says, "I know I won't out run that bear but I might outrun you!"

Survival of the fittest has been one of the main themes that I keep coming across with the businesses that I advise.

If ten businesses are going after that market then on average three of them won't survive.

Here is an example of two clients of mine; they both own restaurants and when I go into one of them he is complaining about the economy, the government, the weather and is doing nothing pro-active to help his business. A few miles away is another similar restaurant and he does not complain, bitch or moan. Instead he is changing his menu, introducing theme nights, a loyalty card and giving his customers great food and service.

Which one do you think is more likely to survive?

Of the two businesses mentioned above which one are you closest to?

If you want to thrive in business, you need to be pro-active and do lots of different things to get repeat sales and find new customers.

Nothing Like A Real Fire

Have you ever had one of those miserable days when you do not want to go anywhere, the weather is wet and windy for the day? You just know it is not going to stop raining? On the first really bad day of winter, there is only one thing for it – light the fire.

There is nothing as comforting as looking at the flames flickering in a real fire. It is even cosier when it is wet and windy outside. Well, enjoy the real fire while you can because it will be legislated out soon. Somebody was telling me that the E.U. wants to ban open fires. Another one of life's simple pleasures – gone. The E.U. are constantly bringing in new legislation. Some of it will affect your business.

It just highlights again that business and life is often about dealing with change.

Look at how the last recent recession has changed things for people and for business. Those who adapt and adjust to the change will survive. It is one of the few positives of this recession. It will be survival of the fittest. The weak ones will not make it. It is a bit like evolution and what happens in nature. Stay still and you die.

I see it with clients of mine. The ones who are flexible and open to change are doing okay. Those standing still are struggling. Make sure that you are still standing when the dust settles.
- What are you doing right now to make sure you survive?
- Are you doing whatever it takes to survive?

If not, why not commit this week to doing something that will help your business make it through.

> **Change is a constant and how we deal with this will determine much about our business. Darwin put it best when he said, "It is not the strongest who will survive but those best able to manage change."**

Groundhog Day

"The new year is the ideal time to have dusted the cobwebs off the brain and be ready to get motoring." I heard that saying a few years ago and it struck a chord.

- Is your business going along on similar lines?
- Is this year going to be a photocopy of last year?
- Stuck in your own version of Groundhog Day?

Let us get the new year off to a positive start. Have you targets sets for the year ahead – targets for sales, profits and a higher salary for yourself?

If you have not set targets, then I strongly encourage you to do so today.

Step one is to know what you did last year. Hopefully you already know but if you do not then… Look at bank statements, invoices out from last year and know your main figures.

Example: Mary had sales of €60,000 last year and a wage of €30,000. She wants to set a sales target of €80,000 which would allow her to take a wage of €40,000.

How is she going to get that increase? Well, it will not happen by itself – she needs a plan. Some extra sales and marketing activities will be needed. There are four main ways she can grow her sales.

1. Sell more of her current services to existing or past clients
2. Sell more of her current services to new clients
3. Sell new services to existing or past clients
4. Sell new services to new clients

Method No. 1: If Mary was a web designer, she may offer her service of 'monthly updates to your website' to more existing customers.

Method No. 2: She could offer the same service to brand new clients.

Method No. 3: She could sell new services to existing clients. Mary might develop a social media service and offer it to existing clients. Or she may offer it to brand new clients.

If you know anything about my approach to marketing, you can guess that I would advise Mary to prioritise 1 and 3 above.

If you have not done so already why not set a sales and profit target for your business? We all want higher sales. Why not go for an increase of 20% (or more if you feel bullish)?

> **Have stretch sales targets which you review on a regular basis and your sales will almost certainly grow. Make sure this year is not a photocopy of last year and avoid 'Groundhog Day'.**

Was Roy Keane Right After All?

I am slow to bring up the topic that split the country in two – I have been putting this off for quite a while. A good friend and myself have agreed never to discuss Saipan again. That is how heated our discussions got. And I generally regard myself as a placid enough individual.

Anyway, amid the Saipan drama, which gripped the country in the summer of 2002, there was one moment which stuck firmly in my mind. When Roy Keane was on his way home, he was interviewed at one of the airports. After all the chaotic arrangements of missing training gear and balls, Keane made one statement which summed up the whole affair

'If you fail to plan, then you are planning to fail.' Roy Keane, Saipan 2002.

That is as true for any business as it is for a sports team.

The importance of clear goals (what you want to achieve and when you want to achieve it) and a plan to achieve it are essential to success given the limited resources (time and money) that any one person can invest in a business. Everything I have said so far may sound obvious and yet when I talk to business owners, many of them seem to suffer from some sort of collective amnesia, when it comes to planning their own businesses. The fact that most of them also have no monthly accounts or any other indicators to tell them how their business is performing only exacerbates the lack of planning.

7 Steps To Planning And Goal Setting For Your Business

1. Decide exactly what you want. This could be a general goal to increase sales. It might be to sort out your website. Or maybe to build a database of past customers and to keep in regular contact with them.
2. Write down what you want.
3. Set a deadline for your main goal.
4. Make a list of everything that you can think of that you are going to have to do to achieve your goal.
5. Organise your list into a plan.
6. Take action on your plan immediately.
7. Resolve to do something every single day that moves you towards your major goal.

Good luck and remember what Roy said, "If you fail to plan, you are planning to fail."

Failing to plan is planning to fail.
Do you have written goals? It is reckoned that
approximately 3% of people in business have written goals
but this includes all the most successful people. If it works
for them, do you think it might work for you?

Would You Open A New Shop Today?

I run courses for start-ups businesses. Some people are looking to open a shop, others are looking at a café, somebody else wants to open a restaurant. Despite what I think about these ideas, I always encourage people to make up their own minds. But I would prefer them to conduct enough market research first. It is better still if they can test the new idea in the real world, dealing with real people and real customers, because that is the best way to test any idea.

Here is a typical conversation I have with one of these start-ups.

"So, what is the average spend in your restaurant?" I asked.

"€8.50," said Joan.

"Where did that figure come from?"

"I'm assuming somebody will have a sandwich and coffee," said Joan.

"Ok, it is better not to assume. How else could you find out?" I asked.

"Talk to a similar business I'm not competing with," suggested Joan.

"Yes, that would be more accurate. How many people will use the restaurant every day?" I said.

"150," said Joan.

"Where did you get that figure?" I asked.

"That's what we need to cover all our bills," said Joan.

"How do you know it won't be 120 or 100?"

"I don't know," she said.

"How could you find out?" I questioned.

"Stand outside a similar business and count the number of customers," said Joan.

The more I work with start-ups, the more I realise that existing businesses have much to learn from them.

With start-ups, I hammer home the importance of market research. I tell them not to make big assumptions. Turn an assumption into a fact.

Take-aways From Your Research

Get a rough version of the product/service in front of a pulse – real people. Learn from what they tell you. Tweak and make it better. Take it back in front of real people. Learn from them. Rinse and repeat.

Existing businesses make so many of the same mistakes with new products, with marketing, big assumptions on what customers want, not enough market research, not enough testing face to face with real people.

Think like a start-up and your business will be better off.

Be careful of making too many assumptions about your business or your customers.
Be like a start-up and do lots of market research.

Father Ted's Business Lessons

Father Ted is one of my all-time favourite comedies. For me, it is up there with Fawlty Towers and Frasier.

The first episodes of Father Ted came out about twenty years ago and just like fine wine and good music, it just gets better with age. 'Kicking Bishop Brennan up the arse,' is one of the many classic episodes. Ted was given a challenge by another priest of kicking his boss, Bishop Brennan, up the arse.

He lured the bishop onto Craggy Island on the pretext of some apparition appearing in the skirting boards and when the bishop bent over to get a closer look, Ted did indeed kick him up the arse, with Dougal there to capture the incident on camera.

Bishop Brennan was in a state of shock and did not realise what had happened to him, so he left the island without getting stuck in Ted.

However, a short while later, the bishop realised what had happened and rushed back to the island to confront Ted. When the bishop challenged Ted that he had indeed, kicked him up the arse, Ted's defence was pure genius and this was his response: "Of course I didn't kick you up the arse, sure you'd kill me!" he said. It does have some semblance of logic to it and the bishop believed him.

And he still believed him until he was getting into a taxi to leave Ted's house, when he saw a massive photograph on the side of the house that Ted had ordered himself, of him kicking Bishop Brennan up the arse. At which point the bishop took his retribution on Ted. Classic stuff.

You may be wondering what this must do with business.

Just like the bishop needed proof before he believed that Ted had actually kicked him up the arse, I find many business owners want proof before they believe.

In the past, while doing some marketing with one particular business owner, she decided a seminar may be a good way of getting her message out to potential customers. I agreed with her and we started putting a plan in place to organise the seminar.

However, a week later, she started getting cold feet and asked me, "How many people are likely to come to this seminar?"

Nobody could answer that question for her as it is impossible to know in advance. I have organised many seminars in the past and I know it takes quite a bit of work to get thirty or forty people into a room. But it is very doable if it is planned in advance. However she wanted to know before putting in the work. And that is not how marketing works.

Marketing is trial and error and you must put in the work first. It may or may not work but there is no way of knowing in advance.

I was not surprised when she said she was cancelling the seminar. It was at that same point that she became an ex-client. I have seen this so often before and I have no interest in working with people who are not willing to put in the work.

Have you ever found yourself in a similar situation, where you're planning to do something but are not sure of the result? How do you respond in that situation? Did you plough ahead, put in the work and then find out if it worked or not? Or did you bail out, not do the work and not get a result.

The most successful businesses I see take the first approach, do lots of marketing and get a result. It is not always positive but when you try many approaches, some of it will work and bring you extra sales.

> **Marketing is trial and error so you must do the work to get the evidence and find out if something works or not.**

Will This Work?

"Will this work?" she asked me.

"Do you think my idea will take off?" another guy asked me.

I had four mentoring sessions in one day, all with start-up businesses. I spent one and a half hours with each person. As a mentor I am there to review, ask questions and give guidance.

Some of these people think I am Mystic Meg. I get asked similar questions by business owners every day, questions around marketing campaigns and sales initiatives. If I could predict the future, I wouldn't be there chatting to them – I would have picked the winning lotto numbers or the winner of the 2.40pm at Haydock Park.

One woman was looking to open a ladies' wear shop; in a decent sized town that did not cater for a certain age category.

"Am I mad?" she asked me. I was only chatting to her for ten minutes at this stage so I could not comment on her mental state. She wanted me to say, 'Yes, go ahead' or 'No, this sounds crazy do not do it.' I have a rule I follow in these situations. And this applies to business owners too. The longer I am working with start-up businesses and stating the importance of market research, the more I realise it applies just as much to existing businesses.

Okay, my rule is this: I never advise people on big decisions. I simply help them to make an informed decision. Questions such as: Should they go ahead with a business or not? Should they close down the business?

My approach in all these situations is similar.

I advise and guide these people to gather enough relevant information so they can make an informed decision.

For example, take the woman who wants to open a ladies' fashion shop. Part of her research is as follows:

We have identified a similar shop in a town twenty miles away. On Saturday, she and her friends will spend the day in a car parked near the shop. They will count all the people who go in. And count the number who have bought something and have a bag.

She knows another similar shop sixty miles away. She will talk to the owner about their average sale. She will get details of the population within a ten- to fifteen-mile radius of her town. She will survey her target market online, by phone and face to face. And do lots of other research.

With all this info, she will be able to estimate her first twelve months' sales. She will know her costs. She can deduct one from the other. And then decide whether to open her shop or not.

Tell me, how much research did you conduct before starting your business? It is never too late to conduct market research.

> **There are no certainties in life.**
> **In business, you need to try lots of things before you find**
> **some that work. Like throwing mud against a wall, most of**
> **it will fall off but some will stick.**

Get the Last Train To...

I got a phone call from a neighbour yesterday evening.

"Do you know when the Muskerry tram stopped running?" asked Pat, my neighbour.

My father was into local history, hence the call. "I think it was 1934 but hold on one second." I said and I grabbed some papers from a drawer and checked a certain page. "29th December 1934."

"I only wanted the year – how do you have the exact date?" said Pat.

I proceeded to tell Pat the story. That date was in my uncle's diary from 1934.

He was on the last ever Muskerry train from Cork City to Tower and on into Blarney. His diary entry for that day was: '*To Cork with Dermot (his brother) on last run of the Muskerry train. Great night's fun. Bus back home. Cards and music in O'Leary's until late.*'

We only found the diary a few years ago after my dad died. It is a great O'Brien tradition, keeping a diary. And I am so glad he did because I never knew my uncle Neil, my father's brother. He died young in 1947. But through his diary, I feel I have gotten to know him. He was a good golfer. He worked in the bar in the local golf club, as I did, while I was in college. I also got a great sense of the lifestyle at the time. Most evenings he would gather with friends and neighbours in somebody's house to tell stories and play cards (no TV or laptops in those days).

Writing Stuff Down Is Very Important.

During one of my training workshops, one of the business owners made the comment, "I have often had sales targets but never wrote them down. Last week, I wrote down my targets for this year and what a difference it made writing them down."

Committing something to paper makes it more real. All of that group have set targets for the year ahead. Targets for sales, profits and their own wage (a bit higher in most cases).

Setting a target is only half the battle. You must measure the actual versus the target on a regular basis. At least monthly but weekly in some cases. The entire training group know this and get it. Hopefully you have done so too. Set targets for sales, profits and your wage for the year ahead. And track it on a regular basis. No more reminders.

When we write something down, we commit to it on a much greater level than just saying it. Get into the habit of writing down important things.

What Can You Do in 5 Minutes?

Ok and before your imagination starts running wild, I am talking about business here.

What can you do in 5 minutes?

- Send an email.
- Make a quick phone call.
- Check the post.

There does not seem a lot you can do in 5 minutes.

This question was prompted by a couple of emails I received. The gist was, 'please only send your emails once a week as I do not have time to read them every day.'

I got two emails like this last week. Maybe you're thinking the same, maybe not. I estimate that it takes less than two minutes to read the daily emails I send. Now if you want or need a bit of time to reflect or think about the message that might take 5 minutes.

Now I am not suggesting for one moment that people have to read my emails. There's lots of good information online and elsewhere. But if you are too busy to stop for 5 minutes, read and reflect on an email, I would have some concerns for your business and time management.

Have you got your head down, beavering away, like the hamster on his little wheel? It reminds me of the story from Steven Covey's great book, the '7 Habits.' A man in the forest was sawing down a tree with a blunt saw. He saws and saws, and saws and saws. Working feverishly but not getting very far. A passer-by suggests he take a break and sharpen his saw. He gets this response, "I don't have time for that."

Are you working away feverishly and not taking time to sharpen your saw?

There are lots of demands on our time, as business owners, and some days there does not seem to be enough hours in the day.
- Just how productive are those days?
- Are we doing tasks that should not be done?

Have you heard of working IN your business and working ON your business?

Working in your business is all of the day-to-day stuff like emails, phone calls, looking after customers. Working ON your business would be planning, reviewing, marketing, training staff or developing your website. You will recognise the ON the business stuff as generally it has no deadline.

What percentage of your week do you spend working ON your business? I would suggest that taking five minutes to read a short email that may have an important message for your business is also working ON your business.

> **Work ON your business as well as IN it.**
> **Do not be like the man sawing for hours with a blunt saw who said he did not have time to sharpen his saw. Take time to stop and sharpen your saw.**

What's Your Favourite Comedy?

I was watching an episode of Frasier and it got me thinking, "What is my favourite comedy?" Fawlty Towers has aged very well and contains some classic catch phrases. Father Ted is not everybody's cup of tea but it is got some hilarious moments (lampooning the movie 'Speed' with Dougal driving the milk float takes some beating).

In my humble opinion, Frasier is up there with the best of them. Frasier and his brother Niles drink sherry and love the opera. They are complete snobs. Their dad loves beer and watching sports. The contrast makes for great comedy. Like all good shows, it follows a formula. The contrast above is part of it.

In many episodes, Frasier meets a beautiful woman and thinks this must be 'the one.' It usually lasts about a week until he insults her or does something to mess things up and he is single again.

Like T.V. Shows, Business Also Follows Formulae.

Successful business people have a formula and approach they follow.

This could be called successful business formulae. Others in business follow different formulae which do not work. This can be called an unsuccessful business formulae. This may sound very simplistic but often we can boil things down to this kind of level. So, being honest with yourself, is your business formula successful or not right now?

If you are not sure, look at your bank account or order book. The amount of sleep or lack or, may also be an indicator.

Here is a simple but powerful statement from George Bernard Shaw:

'The definition of insanity is doing the same thing over and over but expecting a different result.'

If your business formulae are not successful but you are still doing the same things, maybe it is time to change.

I appreciate this can be difficult to take on board and then act on, but the alternative is pretty easy to predict. If something isn't working and you do not change your approach, you will not have a business for too much longer.

Successful TV shows like Frasier have a formula or an approach that works. When it works well, it is called a 'Success formula.' Business is the same. Successful businesses have a formula that works, while unsuccessful ones have an approach that does not work. The good news is that nobody has a monopoly on this success formula in business. And it is not too difficult to find out what it is.

Find successful businesses and watch what they do closely. Then apply what you learn to your business.

The Train and the Steam Roller

You may have seen the photo somewhere. You may have seen it on the wall of a hotel. I have seen it in lots of bars. It is one of the most famous train photos ever taken. It has gone all around the world.

September 6th, 1927. The day a steam roller crashed into a... train. Luckily the train was not going too fast. It wasn't the quickest train in the world. The old joke was you could pick blackberries from it while it was going. My grandfather was on that train. And he kept a diary, giving us a first-hand account of the crash. Yesterday evening I went to a fascinating historical talk on the ancient train. And my grandfather's diary featured prominently. They were building a new road at the time and the steam roller got too close to the tracks. That should be obvious but believe it or not, the cause of the crash is still hotly debated.

It is amazing how firmly we can stick to our beliefs. There are still people who firmly believe the train, going along merrily on its track, was to blame for that crash. Just like there are thousands of people who believe the earth is still flat.

And the train is a pretty good image and one I have used in the past with clients. If you are not happy with some aspect of your business, it is a bit like a train heading along its track. It is heading to the station – maybe the station of being flat broke and unless it can get off those tracks then... If your business is losing money and something does not change then it does resemble that train on its track.

As I mentioned earlier, the definition of insanity is doing the same thing but expecting a different result. Make sure you are not like the train on the track...

205

> **If your business is not giving you the results you want, then like a train on a track, you may be headed in the wrong direction.**

Making Toast on An Open Fire

One night I got a mad notion. I did something I had not done for years. I do not even know how it popped into my head. I had a mad notion to… make toast on the fire.

I realise you may be too young to remember this. This is something we loved doing as kids. You had to wait until the fire died down and the embers were glowing red. We had a long-handled fork and you would stick this into the bread. You had to try to hold the bread over the fire so it would toast but not fall in.

And you tried not to scald your fingers (but they always got very hot). And after about a minute the bread would curl as it started toasting. Because of the heat of the fire the bread would toast very quickly. Then as soon as it was toasted you put butter on and watched it melt. And it was the nicest toast you had ever eaten, so good that you wanted another one straight away. I won't say how many years it has been since I last did that… But I made toast on the open fire that night and it was delicious.

In business, it can be the same. We could have something that worked well, but we have forgotten about it. Too often we're looking for something new to win business and grow sales. Maybe it is our website, social media or even those voucher sites. Not saying there is anything wrong with looking at new methods. But at this stage they may be untested. We do not know if they will work or not.

But there may be something we did before which worked very well. But we have forgotten about it.

Just think for a moment. Where did your best clients come from? What about your biggest orders? What was your most successful marketing campaign ever?

If it worked before there is a good chance it will work again. We do not need to find something new to bring us business. We just need to do something that works.

> **There is something in us that is always looking for the new shiny penny. A bit like the toast from an open fire sometimes we forget the things that have worked before.**

Fairy Tale of New York

I have tried delaying the inevitable as long as I could. But about 7.15pm on a November evening I heard it, the 'Fairy Tale of New York.' The definitive Christmas song. The best Christmas song ever? Yes, no argument.

You see, once I hear that song every year, for me, officially Christmas has started. Not that I do not like Christmas because I do. It just seems to start earlier every year. One year I heard Christmas ads before Halloween. That cannot be right.

I love Christmas, the feeling of goodwill everywhere. Christmas Eve has to be the best day of the year. It is a nice break from work as I always take two weeks off.

Now I appreciate that everybody does not feel the same way about Christmas. Some people hate it. For some it probably stirs up bad memories. For others being thrown together with their family for a few days is akin to a trip to hell. No matter how well families get on, Christmas can be a trying time. But it comes around every year, same as night follows day.

My philosophy on life is that I only worry about the things I can control.

Some people do not like the short days of winter. Others do not like the cold. Therefore, during the crap weather of summer when everybody was moaning and groaning, I just got on with it. There was nothing I could do about it, the government or the budget.

I must admit for a while I did read all about the downturn and the government's actions. I listened to the news and bitched and moaned about the shower of incompetents running the country. After a while I stopped. I realised there is nothing I can do about them. Not that they do not annoy me from time to time, but I tend not to listen to the news or spend too much time worrying about the economy. I am not trying to claim to be superior in any way, but I save my energy and emotions for the things I can control, like my business, and helping my clients and developing new products.

Why not save your time and energy for the things you can control?

It is very easy to worry and stress about lots of things - the government, bad weather etc. That is a lot of energy wasted on stuff you cannot control. Why not save your thoughts and energy for stuff you can control, such as your business?

What Drives Me Nuts

Picture the scene... You're driving along a country road. It is dark, wet and windy. You see a single light coming against you. "Bad night to be on a motorbike", you think to yourself. Until the 'bike' gets closer and you realise... It is not a motorbike! It is a car with no outside light! You have to swerve a little to make sure you do not crash. Sadly, this is not an isolated incident. Every day driving around country I see cars missing lights, missing headlights, missing parking lights, no rear lights.

This is not something new, but it has worsened. How can so many cars be driving around with faulty lights? Because nobody is checking for these things. But you could be stopped by guards twice a month to check your tax disc. A car coming against me without a tax disc won't kill me. But a car with faulty lights could.

Other things that drive me nuts:

1. Politicians making excuses.
2. Inconsiderate people – like the van driver I saw last week who double parked blocking a woman in for ten minutes.
3. The doom and gloom of the media.

Ok, that is my major 'rant' out of the way... We all have things that drive us nuts.

In reality, the things that could drive me nuts actually do not. Because I have an overriding rule that says: only worry about the things I can control.

So there is not much I can do about faulty lights and lying politicians. I am not saying I am an angel. Or that I do not like a good rant from time to time. But for the most part, I can ignore things that could potentially drive me nuts.

Even if something drives us nuts, we can still decide how to react. You may have heard this old saying: 'It is not what happens to you that counts; it is how you react to what happens to you.'

Regardless of what happens to you in business, you can always control how you react. Regardless of what happens in the economy, you can always control how you react.

I have some clients who bitch and moan about the government and say, "How can anyone run a business in this recession?" I have other clients who ignore the government and just get on with trying new ideas in their business.

> **Only worry about those things you can control.**
> **It is not what happens to you that counts, it is how you react to what happens to you.**

Do Not Trust the Experts

I saw a story online and thought it was so good I had to share it with you. It is about a Greek man called Stamatis. He was living in the US and was diagnosed with lung cancer. The doctors gave him six to twelve months to live. He wanted to return home to Greece, to die among friends and family.

This is what happened in his own words:

"I found my friends in the village where I was born and we started drinking wine. I thought, at least I will die happy. Every day, we got together, drank wine and I waited. Time passed and I felt stronger. Nine months came, I felt good. Twelve months came, I felt even better. And now, forty-five years later, I'm still here. A few years ago, I went back to the US to find my doctors but they were all dead."

What a great story!

Before anybody thinks I am advocating drinking lots of wine every day, there are other factors here. The island where Stamatis lives has an age expectancy ten years higher than the rest of Europe. Their diet consists of fish, vegetables and very little processed food. And a daily glass of wine... or two.

Ok, I am sure we all accept doctors get it right most of the time but not always. In fact, I am slow to even use the word expert. Some people have more knowledge on a subject than others. But that does not make them an expert. They have lots of knowledge but that does not mean that they are always right.

Take marketing for example. Marketing is a game of trial and error – some things work and others do not. A marketing expert can guess what might work but there is only one way of finding out. Try it and measure the results. Except most people do not test the results of marketing.

On a survey I conducted last year, almost 50% of people had no marketing tracking method. Now I do not claim to be a marketing expert. But if I did marketing with you, I would test the results. That way we would know what works or does not work. And I would pick ideas that I think may work for you, and try them one by one. And measure the result.

They would not all work. But I keep going until I find some that do work. And those ideas will increase your sales.

> **An expert is somebody who has knowledge on a subject and a process to get results with that knowledge.**

Time Management Is A Load of Crap

Time management and planning, those old chestnuts just won't go away. In the past, I have asked people to send me their top three goals and main three challenges. Over 80% of challenges were around time management and planning. Personally, I think traditional time management is a load of CRAP. It aims to fit a litre into a pint glass.

If you work sixty hours per week, it tries to get you organising yourself better so that you can get the same workload done in fifty hours. The only problem I have with this approach is that it is helping us do more efficiently a lot of stuff that we probably should not be doing at all.

Why? Because it is not that important. There is no point scrambling very efficiently up the ladder of success if it is leaning against the wrong wall.

'*Eat That Frog*' by Brian Tracy and '*The 4-Hour Work Week*' by Tim Ferris are books I love. These books tell us something different. Their message, which I agree with 100%, is that only 20% of what we do is really important and this is what we should do first. The rest can wait and be done later (or maybe not at all).

If we have ten jobs to do, then two of them are more important than the other eight and these should be done first.

If the first thing you do in the morning is eat a live frog, you will have the satisfaction of knowing that it is probably the worst thing you will do all day.

We need to know our most important task and do that first. Do not be tempted to do a few small jobs so we can tick them off our list.

Note: If you can do the task in ten minutes, it is probably not that important. Can you start work an hour earlier? If not, then only work on your most important task first.

A frog could be working on your website, a new product or service, a marketing campaign or training staff. There is a good chance that your frog is not even on your plan for this week (assuming you have a plan). Believe me when I say this can transform your business and life. I have been practicing the 'frog' approach for several years and it has made a huge difference to my productivity.

> **The key to reaching high levels of performance and productivity is for you to develop the lifelong habit of tackling your major task first thing each morning. Prioritising (eating your frog) and focusing on that important task are two keys to getting more done every day. Try them.**

Business Lessons from A Tomato

I must admit this is one title I never imagined writing. Bear with me a moment and all will be revealed.

First comes the context. Have you ever had those days when you have felt you got nothing done? Your day was full of interruptions, and you jumped from one thing to another without completing any?

Well let me introduce the… Pomodoro. No, not the tomato but a work method that may help your day be more productive. Not sure how it got its name but it is called the Pomodoro method.

Here's how it works:

- ✓ **Pick your most important job (often called your frog).**
- ✓ **Work on this for 25 minutes without interruption.**
- ✓ **Then take a 5-minute break.**

Repeat the process four times: working for 25 minutes followed by a 5-minute break.

At the end of the fourth one, take a 25-minute break. It is based on the theory that our brains can concentrate for a fixed period of time and then needs a break.

I have tried this and really like it. The first time I tried it, I found my mind wandering.

'Forgot to send Mary that email,' or 'Must check those sales figures.' But I didn't get distracted. I knew I could do those jobs later. I stuck with my task. I found the 5-minute break gives me a chance to reflect on what I have done.

"How effective was it?"

"Is there a better, easier way to get this job done?"

Why not give it a go and see how you get on?

We have so many distractions these days with emails, smart phones and the Internet. Focusing on your frog task is vital. Use this Pomodoro method to block out these distractions.

The End

Notes and Action Items

Dear Reader,

I would encourage you to make notes as you go through this book
Then make a list of the action items you will commit to and the date of achievement. I have included blank pages for note taking and a lined page with space for up to ten action items.

Notes

Notes

Notes

Notes

Action Items

Action Item	Date
1...	....
2...	....
3...	....
4...	....
5...	....
6...	....
7...	....
8...	....
9...	....
10...	....

Letter from the Author

Dear Reader,

I hope you found *"101 Business Lessons From A Recovering Accountant'*beneficial and that you plan to implement the lessons and strategies contained within this book.

As an author and business professional, I love feedback. Please do take the opportunity to let your voice be heard by contacting me via the links below.

Website: quantum.ie

LinkedIn: neilobrienmarketingconsultant

Facebook: Quantum Business Solutions

If I could ask one more thing, I would really appreciate if you could leave a review of my book on whatever site you purchased it from.

Should you require further support or have any questions, I am here to help and can be contacted at Neil@Quantum.ie.

Bonus Material

1. Complementary Consultation

For a complementary analysis of how 80/20 can impact your business, email Neil@Quantum.ie.

After your consultation you will come away with:
1. Strategies that address your biggest current concerns
2. An initial analysis of how 80/20 impacts your specific business.
3. An action plan that will allow you to focus on activities that produce the best financial outcomes for you..

To make the time most productive and valuable for you, you will be given a short questionnaire once you book your appointment. This will allow me to understand your business at the top level.

2. Private Video and Cheatsheet re-inforcing the key points raised around the 80:20 Principle outlined in this book. (Not found anywhere else). Email Neil@Quantum.ie to get your private link.

3. Profit Tips

Should you also wish to receive a free profit tip every week delivered to your email, go to Quantum.ie.

For any questions or additional support, I can be contacted at Neil@Quantum.ie